# Kindle Survival Guide from MobileReference

## By Toly K

## Table of Contents

# Getting Started

## Table of Contents

# 1. Button Layout

The images below show the Kindle buttons. The general functions of each button are described underneath each image.

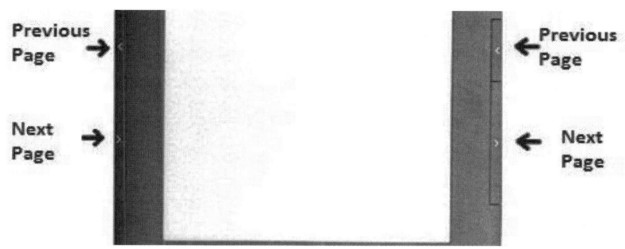

*Figure 1: Navigation Buttons*

**Previous Page Buttons** - Return to the previous page while reading an eBook.
**Next Page Buttons** - Turn to the next page while reading an eBook.

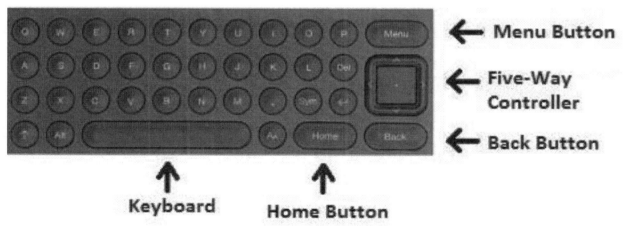

*Figure 2: Keyboard and Menu Buttons*

**Menu Button** – Shows the context-based menu. For example, pressing the menu button in an eBook allows you to jump to a specific page, search the eBook, etc. At the home screen, pressing the menu button allows you to change settings, shop in the Kindle store, and more.

**Home Button** - Shows the Home screen at any time.

**Five-Way Controller** – Functions like a directional pad (up, down, left, right) to highlight options in menus and words in an eBook. Press down on the dot in the middle to select an item (referred to as "push down the five-way controller" throughout this book).

**Back Button** - Displays the previous screen. For instance, if you start reading an eBook from the Home screen, pressing this button will return you to it.

**Keyboard** - Enters text in search fields, notes while reading, or personal information.

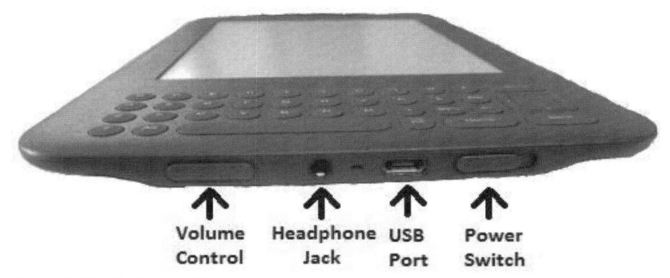

*Figure 3: Kindle Bottom View*

**Power Switch** - Turns the Kindle on and off. Also puts the Kindle in Sleep mode and wakes it up.

**Headphone Jack** – Allows headphones to be plugged in, so that you may use the Text-to-Speech feature to listen to an eBook or to play music.

**Volume Control** - Adjusts the volume of music and Text-to-Speech.

**USB Port** – Allows the USB cable to be plugged in, so that you may transfer content to and from the Kindle and charge it.

## 2. Turning the Kindle On and Off

To turn the Kindle on, slide the **Power switch** to the right and release it immediately. The Kindle turns on. You do NOT need to hold the power switch.

To turn the Kindle off, slide the **Power switch** to the right and hold it there until the green light flashes twice and the screen goes blank. The Kindle turns off.

## 3. Putting the Kindle in Sleep Mode

To put the Kindle in Sleep mode while the device is turned on, slide the **Power switch** to the right and release it immediately. A random image is displayed and the Kindle goes to sleep.

## 4. Charging the Kindle

Charge the Kindle before first use. To charge the Kindle, use the power adapter that comes with the Kindle. This power adapter is made to automatically switch from 120V (US standard) to 220V (European standard) and can be used worldwide. A plug adapter is still required to connect the Kindle's US power adapter to a non-US outlet.

Alternately, you can charge the Kindle using a PC via the Kindle's micro-USB cable.

The first time you plug it in, the Kindle will take about six hours to charge completely. When the device is completely charged, the light next to the USB port socket turns from amber to green.

# 5. Connecting the Kindle to a PC

Connecting the Kindle to a PC allows you to transfer files, such as eBooks, music, and pictures. To connect the Kindle to a PC:

1. Unplug the USB cable from the power adapter that came with your Kindle.
2. Plug the small end of the USB cable into the bottom of the Kindle. Plug the other end into a USB port on your PC (try not to use a USB hub, as it may not be equipped to detect your Kindle).
3. Go to **My Computer**. The My Computer window opens, as shown in **Figure 4**.
4. Double-click the **Kindle removable drive**. The Kindle folders appear.
5. Double-click a folder. The folder opens.
6. Click and drag files into a folder. The files are transferred to the Kindle.

*Note: Files can also be transferred from the Kindle to the PC. Drag and drop files from a folder to your computer to transfer the files.*

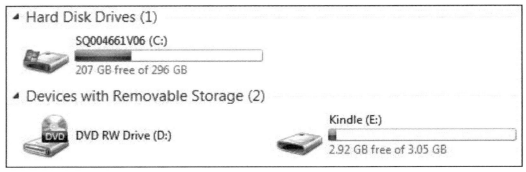

*Figure 4: Kindle Connected to a PC*

# 6. Connecting the Kindle to a Mac

Connecting the Kindle to a Mac allows you to transfer files like eBooks and pictures. To connect the Kindle to a Mac:

1. Unplug the USB cable from the power adapter that came with your Kindle.
2. Plug the small end of the USB cable into the bottom of the Kindle. Plug the other end into a USB port on your PC (try not to use a USB hub, as it may not be equipped to detect your Kindle).

3. Double-click the  icon on the desktop. The Kindle folders appear, as shown in **Figure 5**.
4. Double-click a folder. The folder opens.
5. Click and drag files into a folder. The files are transferred to your Kindle.

*Note: Files can also be transferred from the Kindle to the Mac. Drag and drop files from a folder to your computer to transfer the files.*

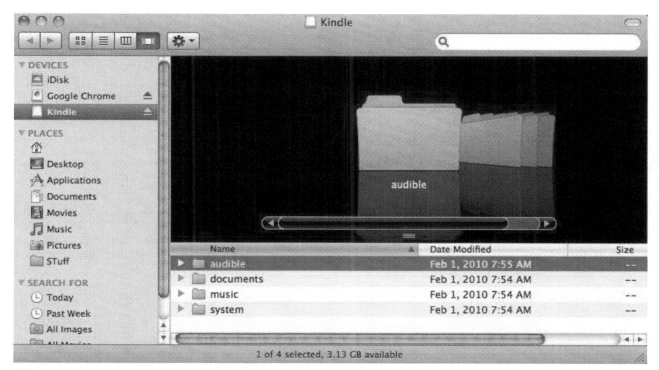

*Figure 5: Kindle Connected to a Mac*

# 7. Registering Your Kindle

Before using your Kindle, you must register it to an Amazon.com account. To register your Kindle:

1. Press the **Menu** button at the Home screen. The Main menu appears, as shown in **Figure 6**.
2. Select **Settings** using the five-way controller and push down. The Settings screen appears. If your Kindle is already registered, your registered name and date appear. If not, the Unregistered screen appears, as shown in **Figure 7**.
3. Select **Register** and push down the five-way controller. The Registration screen appears, as shown in **Figure 8**.
4. Enter your account information using the keyboard. To enter an "@", press the **SYM** button in the bottom row of the keyboard. Navigate through the fields using the five-way controller.
5. Select **Submit** and push down the five-way controller. Your Kindle is registered with your Amazon account.

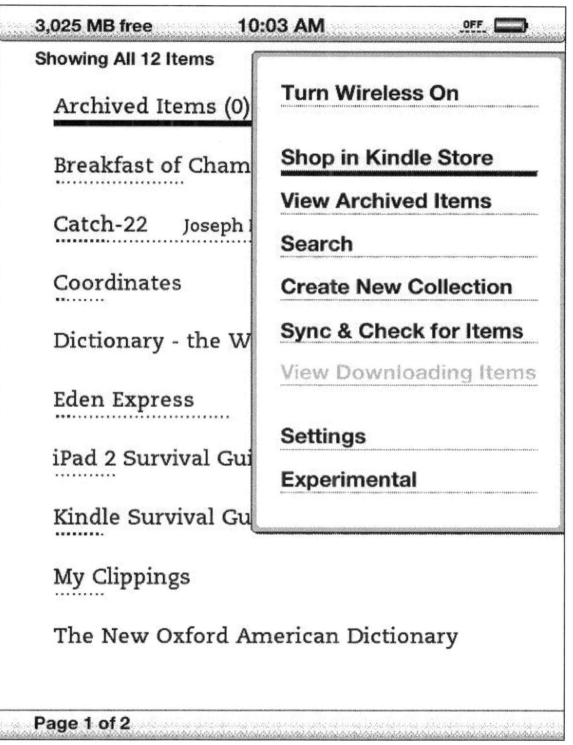

*Figure 6: Main menu*

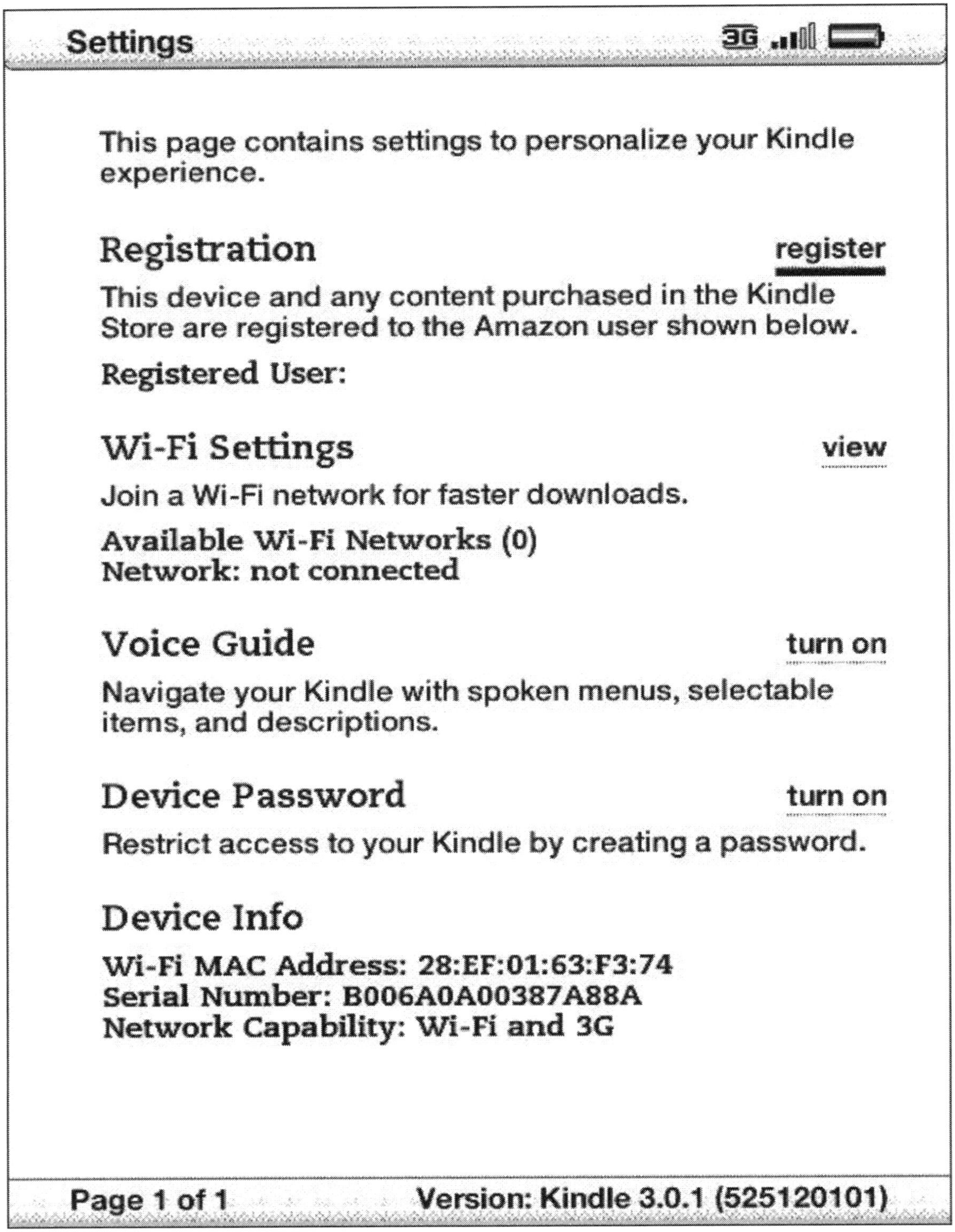

---

**Settings**                                    3G .ull ▭

This page contains settings to personalize your Kindle experience.

## Registration                              register

This device and any content purchased in the Kindle Store are registered to the Amazon user shown below.

**Registered User:**

## Wi-Fi Settings                               view

Join a Wi-Fi network for faster downloads.

**Available Wi-Fi Networks (0)**
**Network: not connected**

## Voice Guide                                turn on

Navigate your Kindle with spoken menus, selectable items, and descriptions.

## Device Password                           turn on

Restrict access to your Kindle by creating a password.

## Device Info

**Wi-Fi MAC Address: 28:EF:01:63:F3:74**
**Serial Number: B006A0A00387A88A**
**Network Capability: Wi-Fi and 3G**

---

Page 1 of 1          Version: Kindle 3.0.1 (525120101)

*Figure 7: Unregistered Screen*

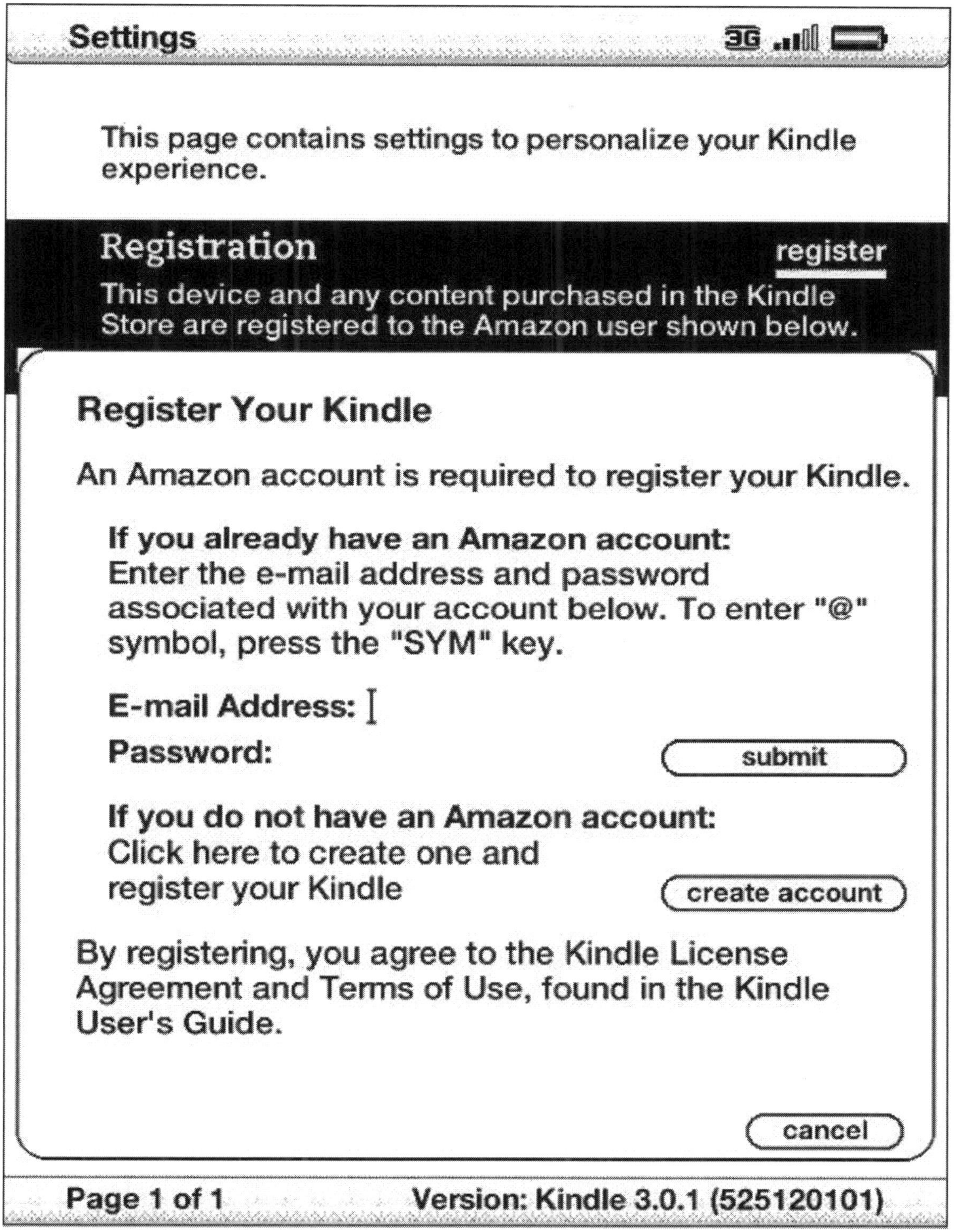

**Settings**      3G ▪▪▪▫ 🔋

This page contains settings to personalize your Kindle experience.

## Registration      register

This device and any content purchased in the Kindle Store are registered to the Amazon user shown below.

### Register Your Kindle

An Amazon account is required to register your Kindle.

**If you already have an Amazon account:**
Enter the e-mail address and password associated with your account below. To enter "@" symbol, press the "SYM" key.

**E-mail Address:** |

**Password:**      ( submit )

**If you do not have an Amazon account:**
Click here to create one and register your Kindle      ( create account )

By registering, you agree to the Kindle License Agreement and Terms of Use, found in the Kindle User's Guide.

( cancel )

**Page 1 of 1**      **Version: Kindle 3.0.1 (525120101)**

*Figure 8: Registration Screen*

# 8. Naming Your Kindle

You may give a name to your Kindle. When purchasing media online, select the name of your Kindle in order to allow the media to be delivered via Whispernet. To change your Kindle's name:

1. Press the **Menu** button at the Home screen. The Main menu appears.
2. Use the five-way controller to select **Settings** and push down on the controller. The Settings screen appears.
3. Select **Edit** next to 'Device Name' using the five-way controller. Push down on the controller. A field appears at the bottom of the screen with the current name highlighted.
4. Type a new name for your Kindle. The new name is entered.
5. Select **Submit** and push down the controller. The new name is assigned to your Kindle.

# 9. Editing Personal Information

You may enter personal information in case you ever lose your Kindle. To edit personal information:

1. Press the **Menu** button at the home screen. The Main menu appears.
2. Select **Settings** using the five-way controller. Push down on the controller to select. The Settings screen appears.
3. Press the **Next Page** button twice. The third Settings page appears.
4. Use the five-way controller to select **Edit** next to 'Personal Info'. Push down the controller. An empty field appears.
5. Enter your personal information, such as your name, address, and/or phone number. The information is entered.
6. Select **OK** and push down the five-way controller. The new personal information is stored.

# 10. Setting Up Wi-Fi

While previous models of the Kindle supported only free 3G connectivity, one of the Kindle 3 models is able to use both Wi-Fi and 3G. To connect to a Wi-Fi network:

1. Press the **Menu** button at the Home screen. The Main menu appears.
2. Select **Settings** using the five-way controller. Push down on the controller. The Settings screen appears.
3. Select **View** next to 'Wi-Fi Settings' using the five-way controller. Push down the controller to select. If wireless is turned off, the Kindle will ask if you wish to turn it on.
4. Select **OK** and push down the five-way controller. A list of available Wi-Fi networks appears, as shown in **Figure 9**.
5. Select **Connect** next to the network to which you wish to connect and push down the five-way controller. The Network Password window appears.
6. Enter the password for your network, if one is required. This password is often found right on the wireless router supplied by your provider.
7. Select **Submit** when finished and push down the five-way controller. The Kindle connects to the network and the network name appears on the Settings screen, as outlined in **Figure 10**.

*Note: If you enter an incorrect network password, the Kindle displays the message "Unable to Connect to Wireless Network".*

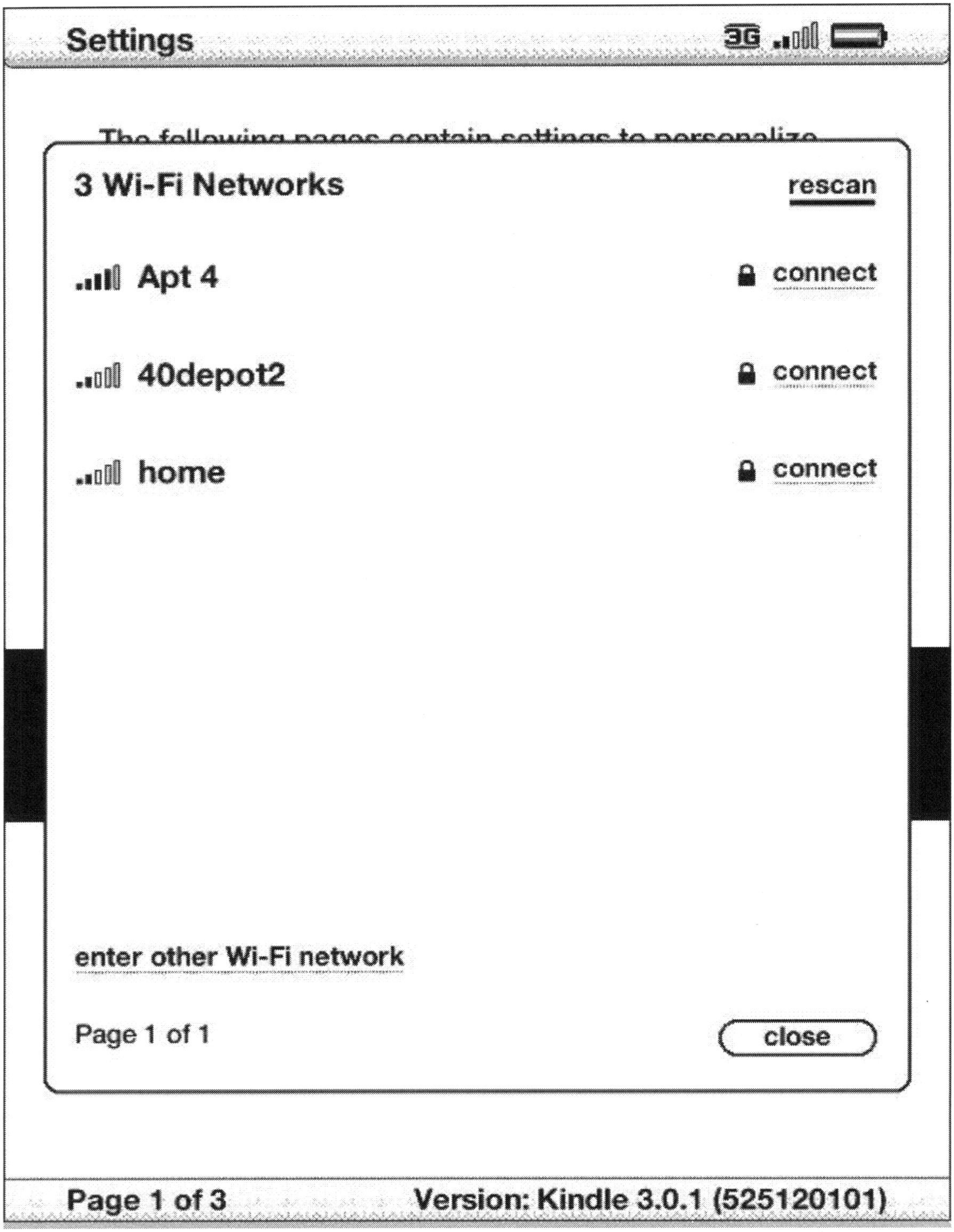

**Settings**  3G ‎‎‎‎‎‎‎‎‎‎ 🔋

The following pages contain settings to personalize...

## 3 Wi-Fi Networks  rescan

.‎‎‎‎‎ **Apt 4**  🔒 connect

.‎‎‎‎‎ **40depot2**  🔒 connect

.‎‎‎‎‎ **home**  🔒 connect

**enter other Wi-Fi network**

Page 1 of 1  ( close )

Page 1 of 3  Version: Kindle 3.0.1 (525120101)

*Figure 9: Available Wi-Fi Networks*

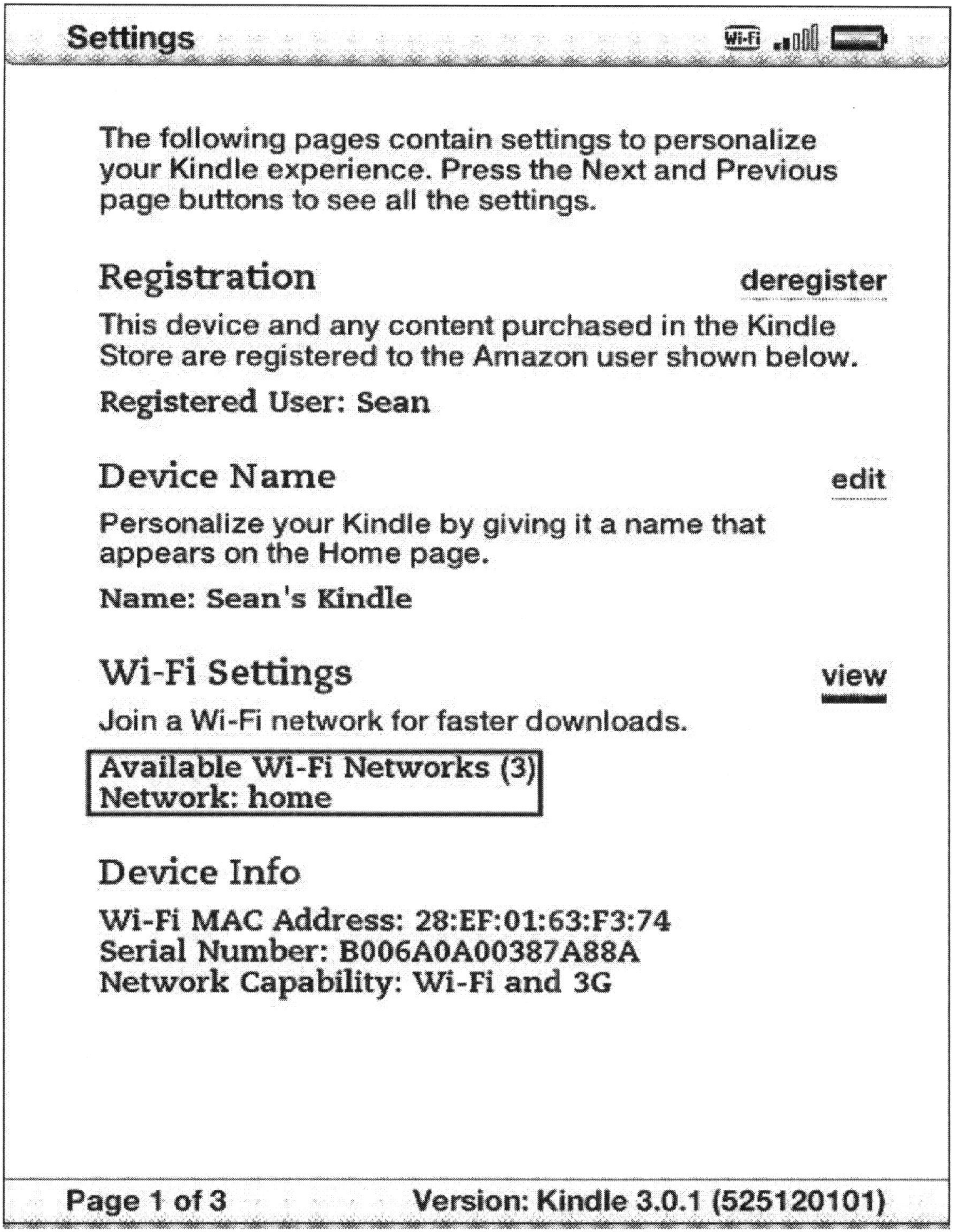

## Settings

The following pages contain settings to personalize your Kindle experience. Press the Next and Previous page buttons to see all the settings.

### Registration                              **deregister**

This device and any content purchased in the Kindle Store are registered to the Amazon user shown below.

**Registered User: Sean**

### Device Name                              **edit**

Personalize your Kindle by giving it a name that appears on the Home page.

**Name: Sean's Kindle**

### Wi-Fi Settings                           **view**

Join a Wi-Fi network for faster downloads.

**Available Wi-Fi Networks (3)**
**Network: home**

### Device Info

**Wi-Fi MAC Address: 28:EF:01:63:F3:74**
**Serial Number: B006A0A00387A88A**
**Network Capability: Wi-Fi and 3G**

Page 1 of 3                    Version: Kindle 3.0.1 (525120101)

*Figure 10: Connected to Wi-Fi Network*

# 11. Viewing and Setting the Device Email

Amazon.com automatically assigns an email address to your Kindle, allowing you to receive documents directly on the eReader. Any documents sent to the Kindle's email automatically appear in the library. To view your Kindle's current email address:

1.  Press the **Menu** button at the Home screen. The Main menu appears.
2.  Select **Settings** using the five-way controller and push down on the controller. The Settings screen appears.
3.  Press the **Next Page** button. The second Settings page appears and your Kindle's email is shown under 'Device Email', as outlined in **Figure 11**.

Your Kindle's email address may be changed to your liking. To change the device email:

1.  Use your computer to navigate to **www.amazon.com/myk**. If you are not logged in, Amazon will prompt you for your login name and password. Once logged in, the Kindle Information screen appears.
2.  Click **Edit Info** under 'Your Kindle(s)'. The device name and assigned email appear.
3.  Type the desired email in the Kindle email address field. Provided that the requested name is not already in use, your new email is entered.
4.  Click the **Update Information** button. The email is updated and automatically appears on the second page of your Kindle's Settings screen.

## Settings

### Voice Guide

**turn on**

Navigate your Kindle with spoken menus, selectable items, and descriptions.

### Device E-mail

You can send documents to your Kindle's e-mail address shown below. To edit the address or add additional addresses to your approved list of senders, go to: www.amazon.com/myk. For UK customers, go to: www.amazon.co.uk/myk.

**dude@kindle.com**

### Device Password

**turn on**

Restrict access to your Kindle by creating a password.

### Device Time

**set manually**

Set the local time on your Kindle.

### Social Networks

**manage**

Share notes and highlights with friends using your social network accounts (like Twitter or Facebook).

### Popular Highlights

**turn off**

Display the passages that are most frequently highlighted by other Kindle users.

**Page 2 of 3**  **Version: Kindle 3.1 (558700031)**

*Figure 11: Second Settings Page*

# Buying eBooks and Other Media

## Table of Contents

## 1. Buying an eBook on the Kindle

You can buy an eBook from the Amazon Kindle Store using your Kindle. To buy an eBook:

*Warning: Before clicking BUY, make sure you want the eBook. The Kindle Store on the Kindle uses one-click purchasing. Once you leave the Confirmation screen, you cannot cancel the order.*

1. Press the **Menu** button. The Main menu appears, as shown in **Figure 1**.
2. Select **Shop in Kindle Store** using the five-way controller. Push the controller down. The Kindle Storefront screen appears, as shown in **Figure 2**.
3. Select **Books** using the five-way controller. Push the controller down. The eBook categories appear.
4. Select a category using the five-way controller and push the controller down. The related eBooks appear.
5. Search for an eBook by typing the title or author and then selecting **Search Store**. To view a subcategory of a list of books, move the cursor to the top right of the screen and select **View Subcategories within...** Navigate to a category by moving the cursor to the top left of the screen. Select a previous category, as outlined in **Figure 3**.
6. Select an eBook. The eBook Description screen appears, as shown in **Figure 4**.
7. Select **Buy** and push down the five-way controller. The eBook is purchased and a confirmation screen appears. The eBook appears in your library.

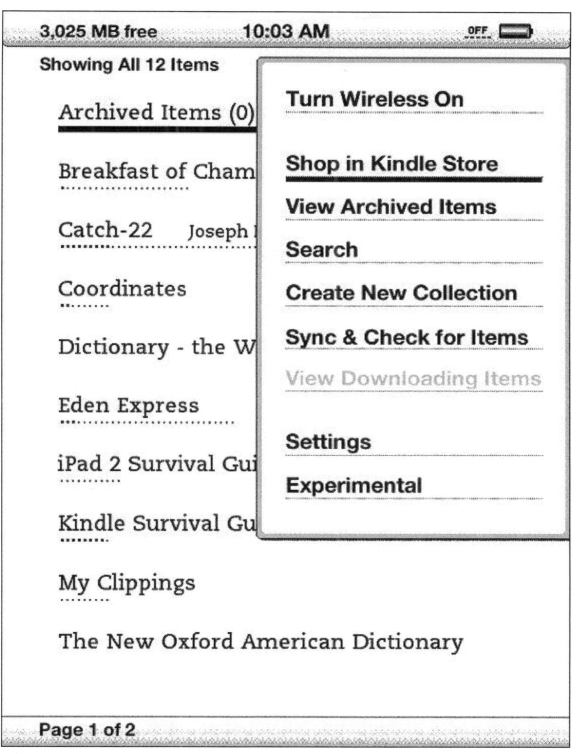

*Figure 1: Main menu*

Sean's Kindle
Wi-Fi
Browse
Books
Audible Audiobooks
Newspapers
Kindle Singles
Magazines
Blogs
Featured
NY Times Best Sellers
Popular Games & Active Content
Kindle Top Sellers
Kindle Daily Post
New & Noteworthy
Things to Try
Thread Words - A Free Word Game for Kindle
SCRABBLE - Play the Popular Word Game on Kindle
Shaken, Not Stirred (Kindle Single) - New Tim Gunn
Recommended for You
VONNEGUT
Kindle Tips, Tricks, and Shortcuts
VONNEGUT
CAT'S CRADLE
See All
Begin typing to search
search store

*Figure 2: Kindle Storefront*

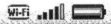

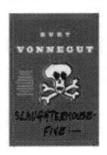

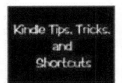

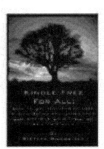

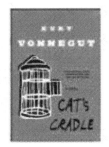

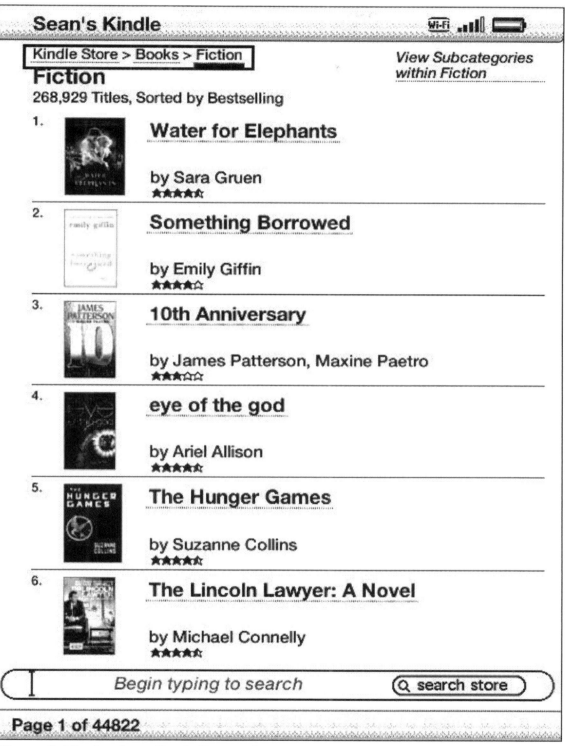

**Figure 3: Navigating eBook Categories**

**Sean's Kindle**  Wi-Fi ▪▪▪▪

# Kindle Survival Guide - Step-by-Step User Guide for Kindle 3: Using Hidden...
*by Toly K*

This Kindle manual gives step-by-step instructions on how to do everything with your Kindle FASTER. You will also unlock hidden secrets on your Kindle, such as how...*More*

Digital List Price: $2.99

Kindle Price: $2.99

**Buy**

Delivery via *Amazon Whispernet*

*Try a Sample*

*Add to Wish List*

★★★⯪☆ 11 Customer Reviews

Sales Rank: #5,904 in Kindle Store
Text-to-Speech: Enabled
Published: Mar 30, 2010
Publisher: MobileReference

Customers who bought this book also bought:

★★★⯪☆ Kindle Shortcuts, Hidden Features,...          *See more*

| Begin typing to search          🔍 **search store**

*Figure 4: eBook Description*

# 2. Buying or Subscribing to a Newspaper

You can buy or subscribe to a newspaper from the Amazon Kindle Store using your Kindle. To buy or subscribe to a newspaper:

***Warning: Before clicking BUY, make sure you want the newspaper issue. The Kindle Store on the Kindle uses one-click purchasing. Once you leave the Confirmation screen, you cannot cancel the order.***

1. Press the **Menu** button. The Main menu appears.
2. Select **Shop in Kindle Store** using the five-way controller. Push the controller down. The Kindle Storefront appears.
3. Select **Newspapers** using the five-way controller. Push the controller down. The Newspaper Category screen appears, as shown in **Figure 5**.
4. Choose a continent using the five-way controller. Push the controller down. A list of all available newspapers for that continent appears, as shown in **Figure 6**. Use the Next Page and Previous Page buttons to scroll through the list of newspapers.
5. Select a newspaper using the five-way controller and push down the controller. The Newspaper Description screen appears, as shown in **Figure 7**.
6. Select **Buy Current Issue** to buy a single issue or **Subscribe now with 14-day Free Trial\*** to subscribe. Push down on the five-way controller. A Confirmation screen appears and the newspaper issue appears in the library on the Home screen. If you subscribed to the newspaper, you have 14 days to cancel your subscription before you are charged for the first time. Refer to "Cancelling Your Newspaper, Magazine, or Blog Free Trial" on page 37 to learn how to cancel your subscription.

*Note: If the newspaper does not appear in your library, it may be because your library is only showing eBooks. If the text at the top of the screen says "Showing ... Books", move your cursor to the top and once to the left. Select **All My Items**. The newspaper issue should now appear.*

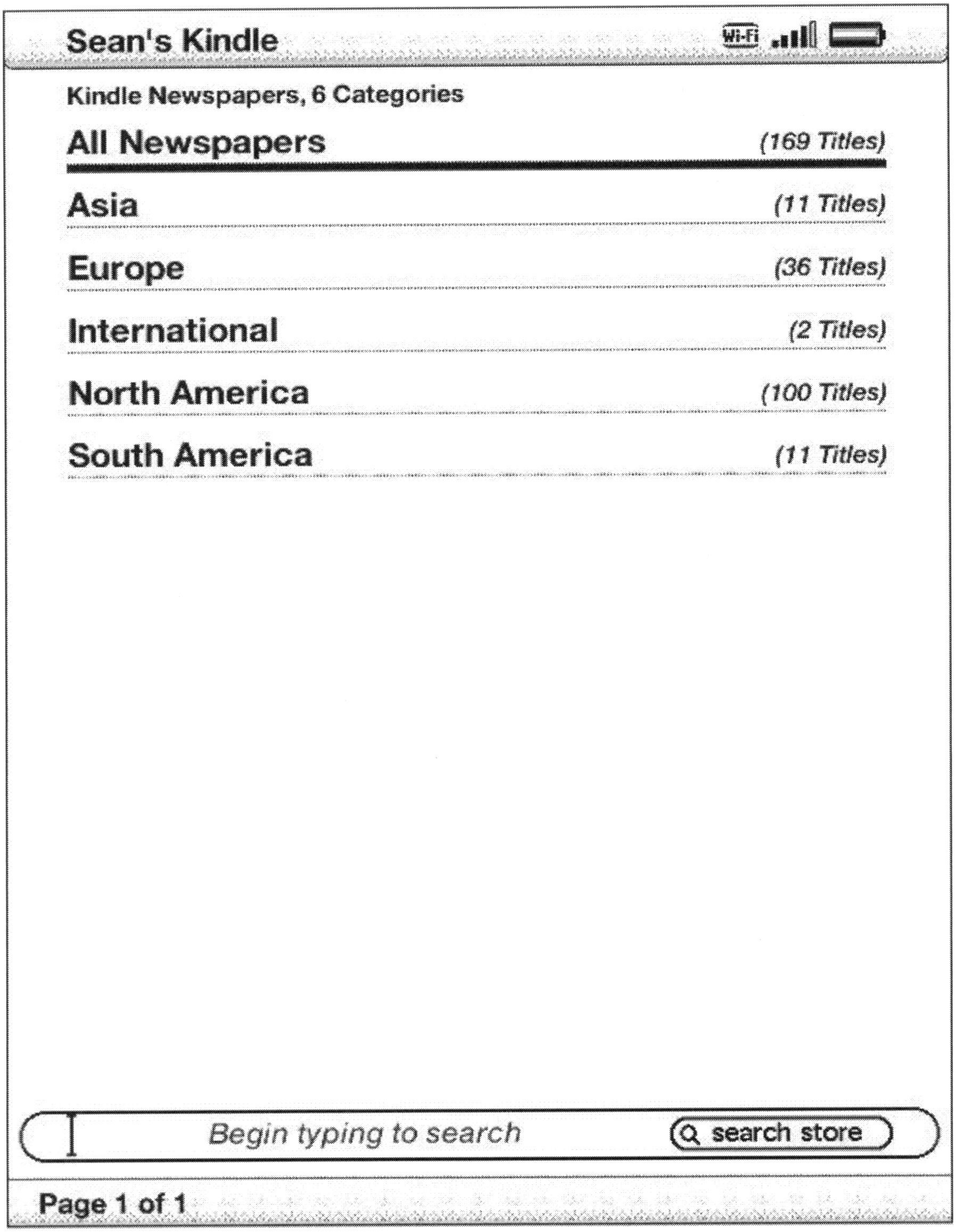

**Sean's Kindle**

Kindle Newspapers, 6 Categories

## All Newspapers                                    *(169 Titles)*

## Asia                                              *(11 Titles)*

## Europe                                            *(36 Titles)*

## International                                     *(2 Titles)*

## North America                                     *(100 Titles)*

## South America                                     *(11 Titles)*

*Begin typing to search*          Q **search store**

**Page 1 of 1**

*Figure 5: Newspaper Category Screen*

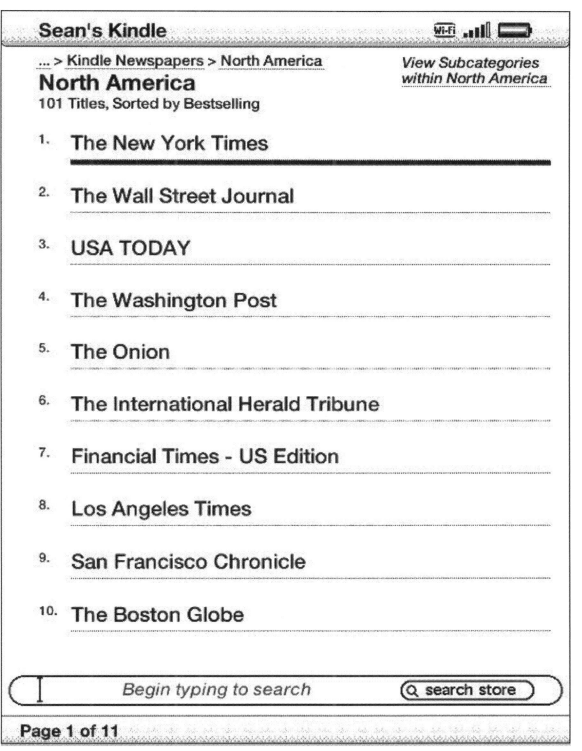

*Figure 6: List of Available Newspapers for North America*

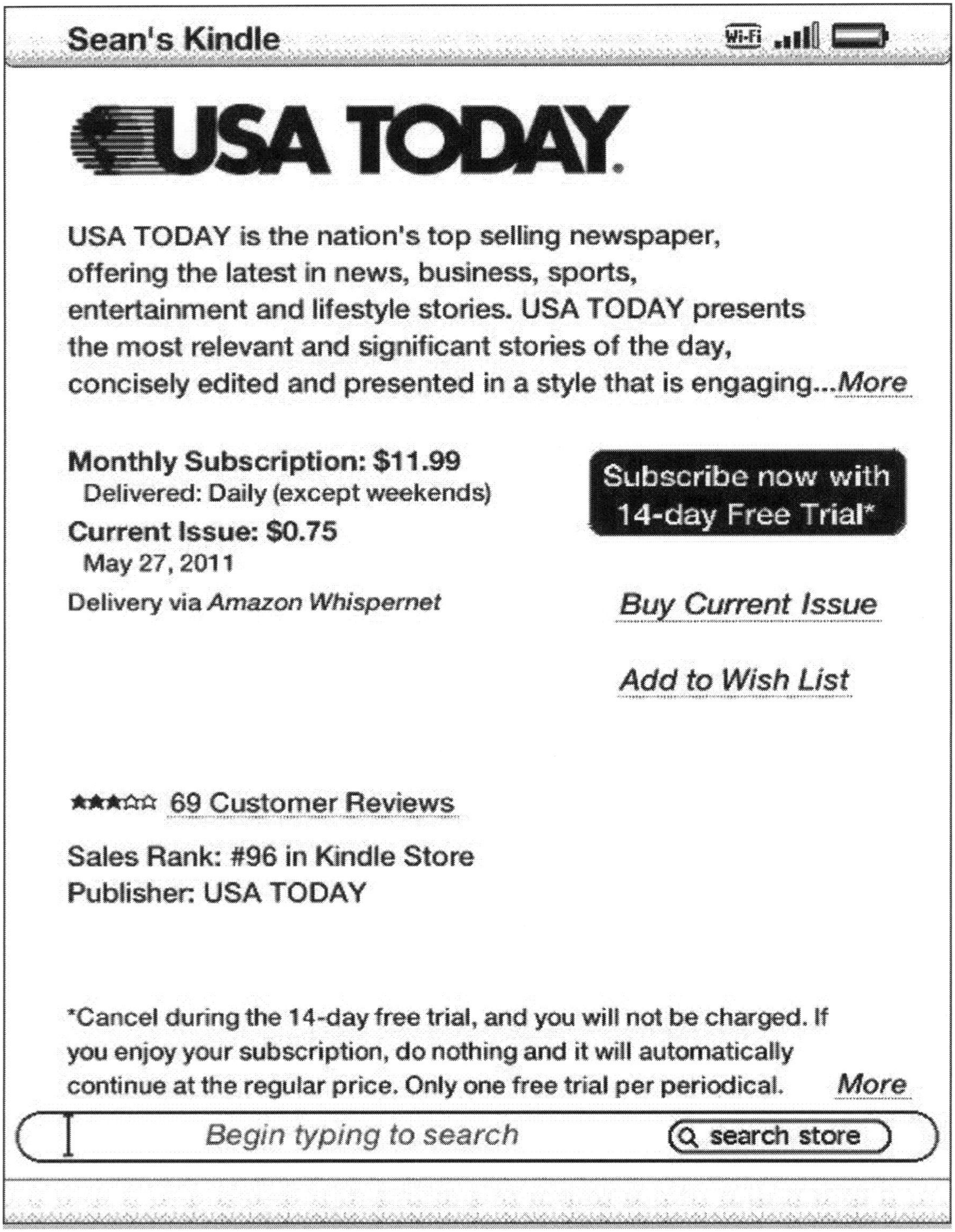

**Sean's Kindle**   Wi-Fi

USA TODAY is the nation's top selling newspaper, offering the latest in news, business, sports, entertainment and lifestyle stories. USA TODAY presents the most relevant and significant stories of the day, concisely edited and presented in a style that is engaging...*More*

**Monthly Subscription: $11.99**
Delivered: Daily (except weekends)

**Current Issue: $0.75**
May 27, 2011

Delivery via *Amazon Whispernet*

**Subscribe now with 14-day Free Trial\***

*Buy Current Issue*

*Add to Wish List*

★★★☆☆ 69 Customer Reviews

Sales Rank: #96 in Kindle Store
Publisher: USA TODAY

\*Cancel during the 14-day free trial, and you will not be charged. If you enjoy your subscription, do nothing and it will automatically continue at the regular price. Only one free trial per periodical. *More*

*Begin typing to search*          🔍 search store

*Figure 7: Newspaper Description*

# 3. Buying or Subscribing to a Magazine

You can buy or subscribe to a magazine from the Amazon Kindle Store using your Kindle. To buy or subscribe to a magazine:

***Warning: Before clicking BUY, make sure you want the magazine. The Kindle Store on the Kindle uses one-click purchasing. Once you leave the Confirmation screen, you cannot cancel the order.***

1. Press the **Menu** button. The Main menu appears.
2. Select **Shop in Kindle Store** using the five-way controller. Push the controller down. The Kindle Storefront appears.
3. Select **Magazines** using the five-way controller. Push down on the five-way controller. A list of all available magazine categories appears, as shown in **Figure 8**.
4. Choose a magazine using the five-way controller. Press the **Next Page** button and **Previous Page** button to navigate the list of magazines.
5. Select a magazine using the five-way controller and push down. The magazine description appears, as shown in **Figure 9**.
6. Select **Buy Current Issue** or **Subscribe now with 14-day Free Trial\*** using the five-way controller. Push down on the five-way controller. A confirmation screen appears and the magazine issue appears in the library on the Home screen. If you subscribed to the magazine, you have 14 days to cancel your subscription before you are charged for the first time. Refer to "Cancelling Your Newspaper, Magazine, or Blog Free Trial" on page 37 to learn how to cancel your subscription.

*Note: If you don't see the magazine in your library, it may be because your library is only showing eBooks. If the text at the top of the screen says "Showing ... Books", move your cursor to the top and once to the left. Select **All My Items**. The magazine issue should now appear.*

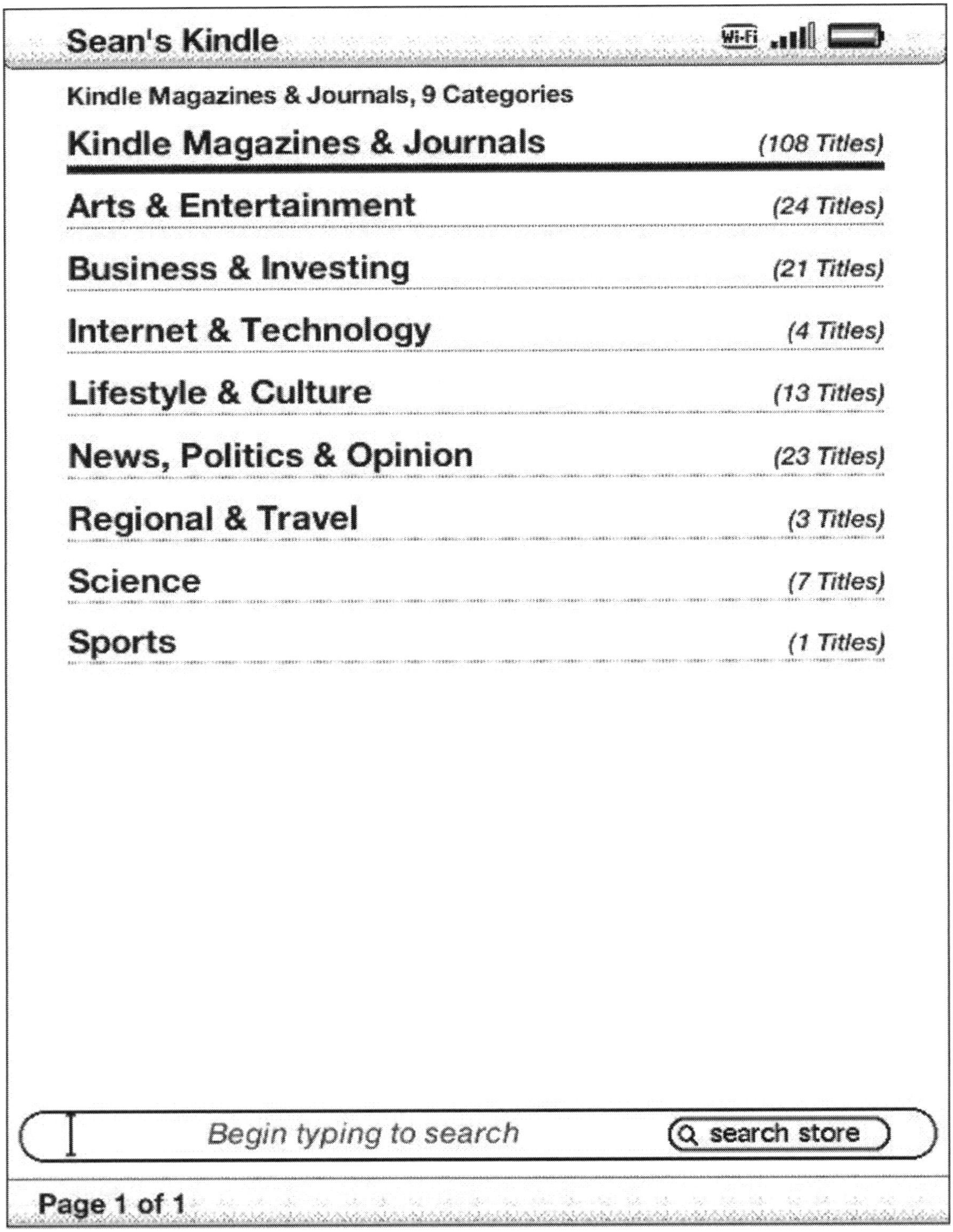

Sean's Kindle      Wi-Fi .ıll ▭

Kindle Magazines & Journals, 9 Categories

| | |
|---|---|
| **Kindle Magazines & Journals** | *(108 Titles)* |
| **Arts & Entertainment** | *(24 Titles)* |
| **Business & Investing** | *(21 Titles)* |
| **Internet & Technology** | *(4 Titles)* |
| **Lifestyle & Culture** | *(13 Titles)* |
| **News, Politics & Opinion** | *(23 Titles)* |
| **Regional & Travel** | *(3 Titles)* |
| **Science** | *(7 Titles)* |
| **Sports** | *(1 Titles)* |

*Begin typing to search*      Q **search store**

Page 1 of 1

*Figure 8: Magazine Categories*

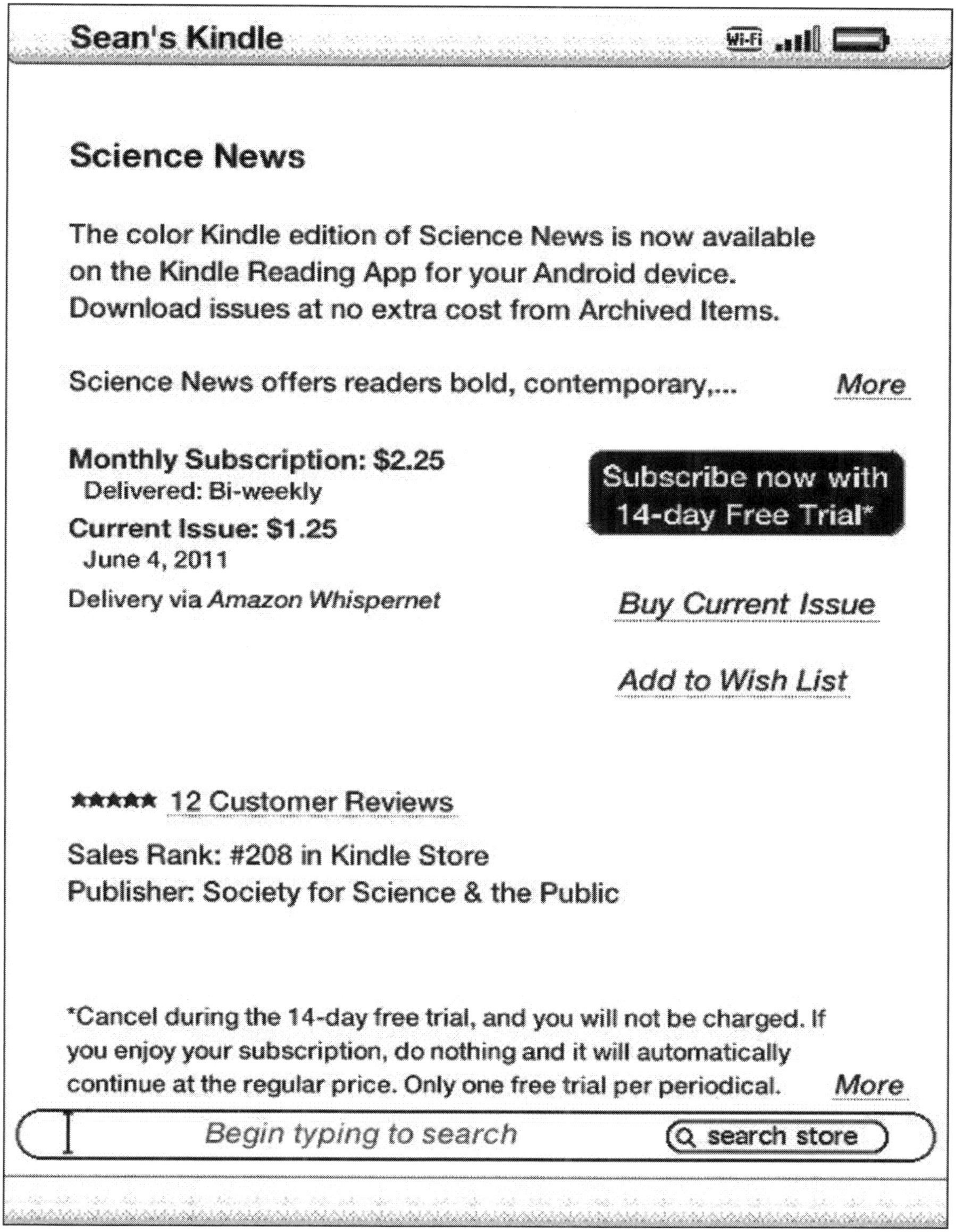

**Sean's Kindle**

## Science News

The color Kindle edition of Science News is now available on the Kindle Reading App for your Android device. Download issues at no extra cost from Archived Items.

Science News offers readers bold, contemporary,...    *More*

**Monthly Subscription: $2.25**
  Delivered: Bi-weekly
**Current Issue: $1.25**
  June 4, 2011
Delivery via *Amazon Whispernet*

Subscribe now with 14-day Free Trial*

*Buy Current Issue*

*Add to Wish List*

★★★★★ 12 Customer Reviews

Sales Rank: #208 in Kindle Store
Publisher: Society for Science & the Public

*Cancel during the 14-day free trial, and you will not be charged. If you enjoy your subscription, do nothing and it will automatically continue at the regular price. Only one free trial per periodical.    *More*

*Begin typing to search*    Q search store

*Figure 9: Magazine Description*

# 4. Subscribing to a Blog

You can subscribe to a blog from the Amazon Kindle Store using your Kindle. To subscribe to a blog:

*Warning: Before clicking SUBSCRIBE, make sure you want the blog subscription. The Kindle Store on the Kindle uses one-click purchasing. Once you leave the Confirmation screen, you cannot cancel the order.*

1. Press the **Menu** button. The Main menu appears.
2. Select **Shop in Kindle Store** using the five-way controller. Push the controller down. The Kindle Storefront appears.
3. Select **Blogs** using the five-way controller. Push down on the controller. A list of all blog categories appears, as shown in **Figure 10**.
4. Choose a blog category using the five-way controller. You can also select 'All Blogs' to view all available blogs. Press the **Next Page** button and **Previous Page** button to navigate the list of blogs.
5. Select a blog and push down on the five-way controller. The Blog Description screen appears, as shown in **Figure 11**.
6. Select **Subscribe now with 14-day Free Trial\*** using the five-way controller. Push down on the five-way controller. A confirmation screen appears and the blog appears in the library on the Home screen. You have 14 days to cancel your subscription before you are charged for the first time. Refer to next section on page 37, "Canceling Your Newspaper, Magazine, or Blog Free Trial" to learn how to cancel your subscription.

*Note: If you don't see the blog in your library, it may be because your library is only showing eBooks. If the text at the top of the screen says "Showing ... Books", move your cursor to the top and once to the left. Select **All My Items**. The blog issue should now appear.*

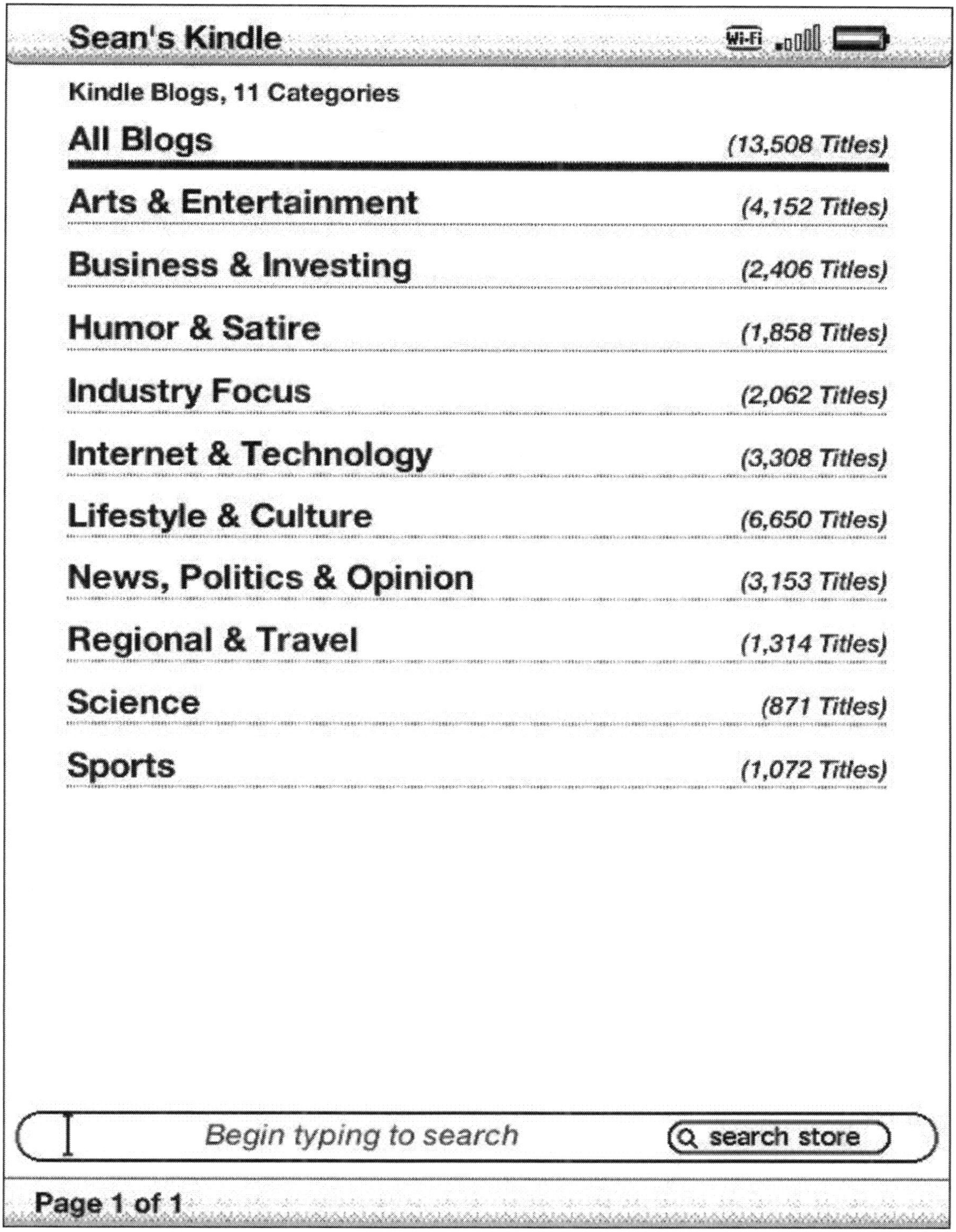

**Sean's Kindle**                                        Wi-Fi .₀₀₀ll 🔋

Kindle Blogs, 11 Categories

**All Blogs**                                            *(13,508 Titles)*

**Arts & Entertainment**                                 *(4,152 Titles)*

**Business & Investing**                                 *(2,406 Titles)*

**Humor & Satire**                                       *(1,858 Titles)*

**Industry Focus**                                       *(2,062 Titles)*

**Internet & Technology**                                *(3,308 Titles)*

**Lifestyle & Culture**                                  *(6,650 Titles)*

**News, Politics & Opinion**                             *(3,153 Titles)*

**Regional & Travel**                                    *(1,314 Titles)*

**Science**                                              *(871 Titles)*

**Sports**                                               *(1,072 Titles)*

| *Begin typing to search* | Q search store |

Page 1 of 1

*Figure 10: List of Blog Categories*

**Sean's Kindle**

Often mistaken for real journalism, The Onion features fact-based, fictional parodies about national and international news. A non-satirical entertainment section covering all aspects of the industry is offered, plus information, critique, and commentary about media and... *More*

**Monthly Subscription: $1.99**
Delivery via *Amazon Whispernet*

**Subscribe now with 14-day Free Trial***

*Add to Wish List*

★★★☆☆ 20 Customer Reviews

**Sales Rank: #915 in Kindle Store**
**Publisher: The Onion**

*Cancel during the 14-day free trial, and you will not be charged. If you enjoy your subscription, do nothing and it will automatically continue at the regular price. Only one free trial per periodical. *More*

| *Begin typing to search* | Q search store |

*Figure 11: Blog Description Screen*

# 5. Cancelling Your Newspaper, Magazine, or Blog Free Trial

To cancel a subscription to a newspaper, magazine, or blog, use the Amazon website. A subscription cannot be cancelled from your Kindle. To cancel a subscription:

1. Go to **www.amazon.com** using your computer's internet browser. The Amazon storefront appears, as shown in **Figure 12**.
2. Click **Your Account** at the top right of the screen. The Login screen appears if you are not logged in.
3. Enter your email address and password. The Your Account screen appears.
4. Scroll down to the 'Digital Content' section on the Your Account screen. Click **Manage Your Kindle**, as outlined in **Figure 13**. The Kindle Management screen appears.
5. Click **Subscription Settings** on the left side of the screen. The Active Subscription screen appears, as shown in **Figure 14**.
6. Click **Actions**. The Subscription options appear.
7. Click **Cancel Subscription**. A confirmation window appears.
8. Click **Cancel Subscription**. The subscription is cancelled.

*Figure 12: Amazon Storefront*

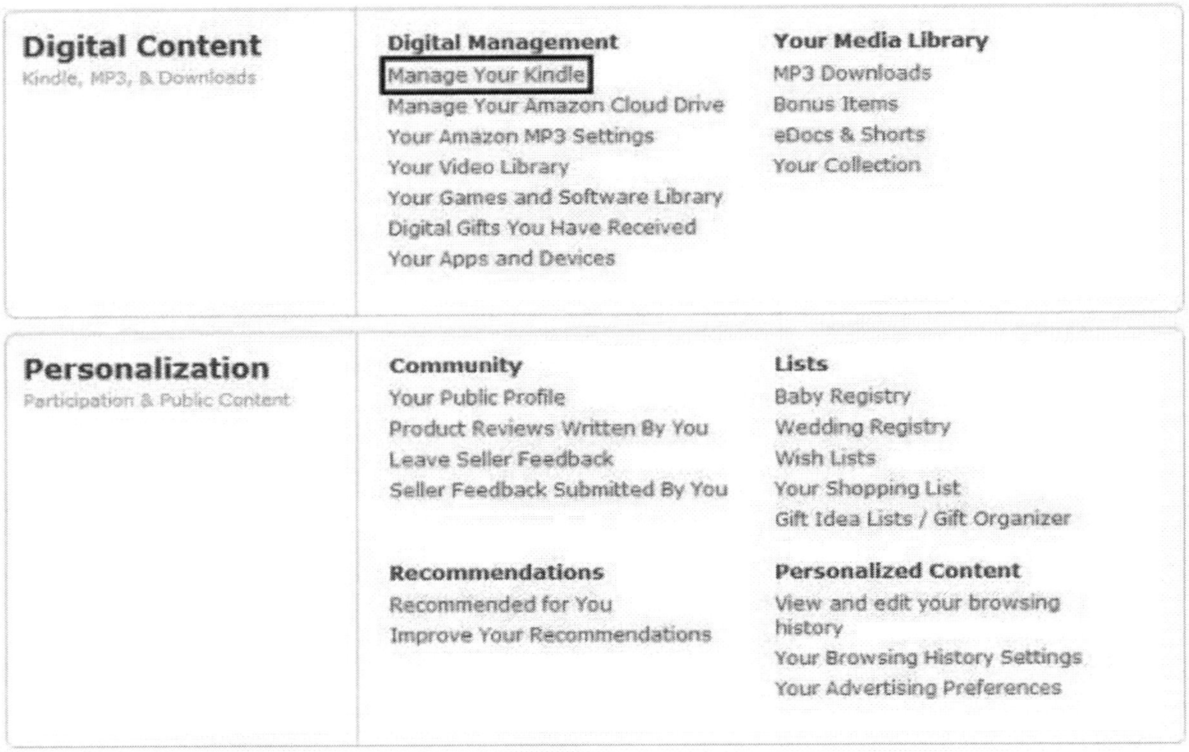

**Digital Content**
Kindle, MP3, & Downloads

**Digital Management**
Manage Your Kindle
Manage Your Amazon Cloud Drive
Your Amazon MP3 Settings
Your Video Library
Your Games and Software Library
Digital Gifts You Have Received
Your Apps and Devices

**Your Media Library**
MP3 Downloads
Bonus Items
eDocs & Shorts
Your Collection

**Personalization**
Participation & Public Content

**Community**
Your Public Profile
Product Reviews Written By You
Leave Seller Feedback
Seller Feedback Submitted By You

**Recommendations**
Recommended for You
Improve Your Recommendations

**Lists**
Baby Registry
Wedding Registry
Wish Lists
Your Shopping List
Gift Idea Lists / Gift Organizer

**Personalized Content**
View and edit your browsing history
Your Browsing History Settings
Your Advertising Preferences

*Figure 13: Amazon Your Account Screen*

**Subscription Settings**

Showing 1 - 1 of 1 active subscriptions

| Title | Billing/Payment | Deliver future editions to | |
|---|---|---|---|
| ⊕ The New York Times | $19.99 Monthly Visa ***3891 Edit | 2nd Kindle | Actions... ▼ |

View inactive subscriptions

*Figure 14: Active Kindle Subscriptions*

# 6. Browsing Recommendations

Amazon makes recommendations based on the media you have viewed or purchased. To look at these recommendations:

1. Press the **Menu** button. The Main menu appears.
2. Select **Shop in Kindle Store** using the five-way controller. Push the controller down. The Kindle Storefront appears.
3. Select **See All** under 'Recommended for You' using the five-way controller. Push the controller down. A list of all browsing recommendations appears, as shown in **Figure 15**.
4. Press the **Next Page** button and **Previous Page** button to navigate the list of recommendations. The recommendations appear.
5. Select an eBook using the five-way controller. The eBook description appears.

**Sean's Kindle**  Wi-Fi ▪▫▫▫ 🔋

# Recommendations

24 Titles

1. ### Slaughterhouse-Five: A Novel

   by Kurt Vonnegut
   ★★★★☆

2. ### Kindle Tips, Tricks, and Shortcuts

   by Michael Gallagher
   ★★★☆☆

3. ### KINDLE FREE FOR ALL: How to Get Millions of Free Kindle Books and Other...

   by Stephen Windwalker
   ★★★★☆

4. ### Cat's Cradle: A Novel

   by Kurt Vonnegut
   ★★★★☆

5. ### Kindle Shortcuts, Hidden Features, Kindle-Friendly Websites, Free eBooks &...

   by Aaron Steinhardt PhD
   ★★★☆☆

6. ### Kindle 3 - the Very Fast Guide to Enjoying It All - free books, the browser, email, and...

   by Don Ursem
   ★★★★☆

| *Begin typing to search* | Q search store |

**Page 1 of 4**

*Figure 15: List of Recommendations*

# 7. Buying an eBook on Amazon.com Using Your Computer

In addition to using the Kindle, eBooks can be purchased online on Amazon using your PC or Mac. To search for and purchase an eBook on Amazon.com:

1. Go to **www.amazon.com** using your computer's internet browser.
2. Click **Books** on the left side of the screen to browse eBooks. The book categories appear, as outlined in **Figure 16**.
3. Click **Kindle eBooks**. The Kindle Store opens and the eBook categories appear on the left side of the screen.
4. Click a genre in the Books menu on the left side of the screen. Keep clicking genres on the left side on the following screens. A list of eBooks is shown each time. Search for a specific eBook or author by clicking on the Search drop-down menu.
5. Click the eBook you wish to purchase. The eBook Description screen appears.
6. Select the name of your Kindle from the 'Deliver to' drop-down menu. Your Kindle is selected.
7. Click **Buy now with 1-Click**. A confirmation screen appears and the item is delivered to your Kindle.

*Note: A purchased eBook is automatically delivered to all devices registered under the email you used to log in to Amazon when purchasing the eBook.*

*Figure 16: Browsing eBooks on Amazon.com*

# 8. MobileReference eBooks

The quality of Kindle eBooks varies greatly between publishers. MobileReference only publishes books that are carefully checked for accuracy and completeness by a team of experts.

**The MobileReference Active Table of Contents**

Looking for a poem or a story on an electronic device in an eBook that contains hundreds of stories is greatly aided by an Active Table of Contents. The Active Table of Contents provides quick access to eBook contents via hyperlinks. Automatically scanned eBooks lack an Active Table of Contents and links to footnotes. MobileReference editors carefully examine each eBook and insert links to individual stories, poems, letters, and footnotes to improve the reading experience and simplify electronic eBook navigation. The result is high quality books with an Active Table of Contents. **Figure 17** shows an example of an Active Table of Contents on the Kindle.

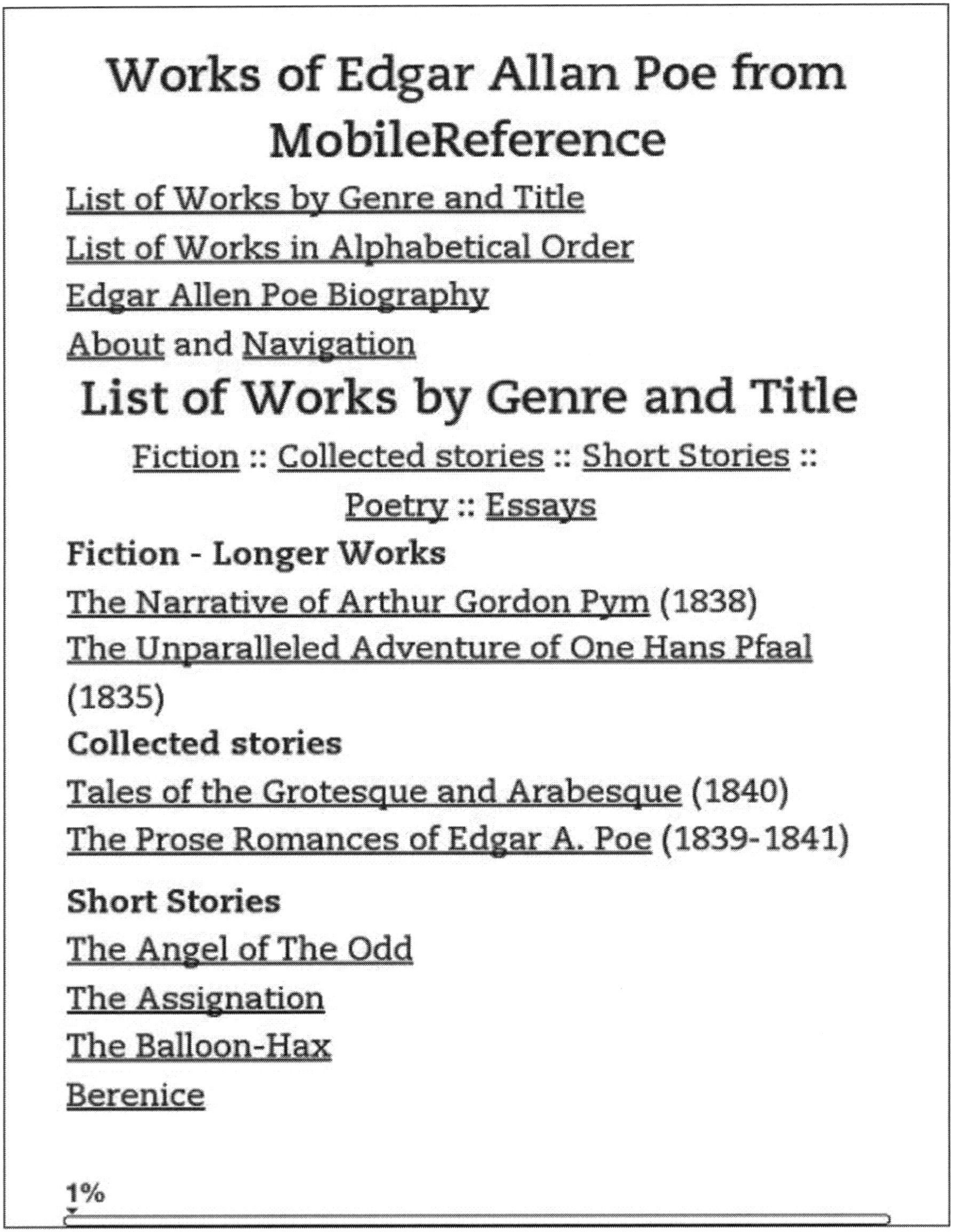

# Works of Edgar Allan Poe from MobileReference

List of Works by Genre and Title

List of Works in Alphabetical Order

Edgar Allen Poe Biography

About and Navigation

## List of Works by Genre and Title

Fiction :: Collected stories :: Short Stories ::

Poetry :: Essays

**Fiction - Longer Works**

The Narrative of Arthur Gordon Pym (1838)

The Unparalleled Adventure of One Hans Pfaal (1835)

**Collected stories**

Tales of the Grotesque and Arabesque (1840)

The Prose Romances of Edgar A. Poe (1839-1841)

**Short Stories**

The Angel of The Odd

The Assignation

The Balloon-Hax

Berenice

1%

*Figure 17: Active Table of Contents on the Kindle*

## MobileReference Author Collections

MobileReference also pioneered the publication of author-collected works in one eBook. This was motivated in part by an effort to reduce the clutter of titles in a digital library. Consider the 'Works of Charles Dickens', which contains over 200 works. When purchased individually, each eBook has an entry in your digital library (analogous to a spine of a paper book). To select an eBook in a digital library of 200 books, one needs to scroll through as many as 20 pages of the library (when ten books are presented on each page). MobileReference author collections organize all eBooks into one electronic volume that has a single representation in a digital library: 'Works of Charles Dickens'.

Inside author collections, MobileReference editors diligently create categorical, alphabetical, and chronological eBook indices. For example, a reader looking for 'A Christmas Carol' can click Fiction > 'A Christmas Carol'. Alternatively, a reader can click 'List of works in alphabetical order' > 'C' > 'A Christmas Carol'. If a reader forgets the book title but remembers that 'A Christmas Carol' was written by Charles Dickens early in his career, he or she can click on the 'List of works in chronological order' > (1843) 'A Christmas Carol'.

By 2011, MobileReference had developed over two hundred collections by Shakespeare, Jane Austen, Mark Twain, Conan Doyle, Jules Verne, Dickens, Tolstoy, and other authors. If you do not see the eBook you want, please email us: support@soundtells.com (MobileReference is an imprint of SoundTells, LLC).

MobileReference author collections cost $5.99 or less.

To search for MobileReference eBooks: enter mobi (shortened MobileReference) and a keyword; for example: mobi Dickens

# Finding Free eBooks

Here is a list of websites offering free eBooks. Please note that only PRC books can be added to the Kindle library. For other file types, please use a computer or other eReader to view the eBook.

## Table of Contents

# 1. Arthur's Classic Novels

**Web address:** http://arthurclassicnovels.com

**Number of available books:** 4000
**Categories:** 20th Century classics, Philosophy, Religion, History, Technology, Mystery, Children's, and many more
**Prominent authors:** Jules Verne, Charles Dickens, Friedrich Nietzsche, Ralph Waldo Emerson, Fyodor Dostoyevsky, and more
**Available formats:** HTML
**How to use:** Search by title or author or browse by category. Click on a title to view it on a separate web page. Use the next and previous page buttons to scroll by page.
**Additional Tips:** There are no eBooks available for download from this website. However, to read an eBook, wireless is not required. Load up the web page containing the eBook and turn wireless off to preserve battery life.

# 2. Baen Free Library

**Web address:** http://www.baen.com/library

**Number of available books:** 100
**Categories:** Science fiction
**Prominent authors:** John Joseph Adams, David Friedman, Richard Roach, and more
**Available formats:** Kindle/Mobi/Palm (PRC), Nook/Stanza (ePub), Microsoft Reader, Sony Digital, RTF, and HTML
**How to use:** Browse by series, authors, or titles by clicking an option on the left side of the screen. Click an eBook to view its description and then download a zipped or unzipped file. Click 'Read Online' to view the HTML version of the book. Click 'Email book to my Kindle' to send the eBook to your Kindle email. The charge is 15 cents per each megabyte. For example, emailing a ten-megabyte eBook to the Kindle costs $1.50.
**Additional Tips:** Several reader programs are available for download on Baen. Download the Microsoft Reader, Mobipocket Reader, and Rocket eBook here.

# 3. BeBook Catalog

**Web address:** http://mybebook.com/download_free_ebook

**Number of available books:** 20,000
**Categories:** Various
**Prominent authors:** Leonardo da Vinci, Sunzi, Arthur Conan Doyle, Jane Austen, William Shakespeare, and more
**Available formats:** Plain text (TXT), PDF
**How to use:** Click a letter to browse by author or title. Click a title to view its description. Click 'download' next to 'Plain text' or 'PDF' to download an eBook. Most eReaders and other devices can open PDF files.
**Additional Tips:** To browse books in another language, click the arrow next to 'Please select language'. After choosing a language, a list of the available books in that language appears.

# 4. Bookyards Library

**Web address:** http://www.bookyards.com

**Number of available books:** 17,000
**Categories:** Classics
**Prominent authors:** Geoffrey Chaucer, Confucius, Robert Burns, Hans Christian Andersen, Julius Caesar, and more
**Available formats:** PDF
**How to use:** Click a letter to browse by title, author, or biography. Click a title to view the eBook description. Click 'Download' to download the eBook.
**Additional Tips:** Many external links are provided under each author. The extra websites are excellent resources for additional free eBooks.

# 5. Christian Classics Ethereal Library

**Web address:** http://www.ccel.org

**Number of available books:** 1200
**Categories:** Christian
**Prominent authors:** Various
**Available formats:** Plain text (TXT), HTML, PDF ($2.95)
**How to use:** Click 'Browse' to peruse the authors, titles, subjects, and languages. Click an author to view the available titles. Click a title to view its description. Click one of the formats to download the eBook.
**Additional Tips:** This website has its own online reader, which is similar to an electronic reader. Click the hyperlinks in each eBook to navigate to another excerpt. Books are available in 13 languages.

# 6. E-Books Directory

**Web address:** http://www.e-booksdirectory.com

**Number of available books:** 4600
**Categories:** Educational, Business, Engineering, Law, Medicine, Nature, Travel
**Prominent authors**: Various
**Available formats:** Various (see 'Additional Tips')
**How to use:** Click a genre. A list of related books appears. Click a title. The title description appears. Click 'Download' or 'Read' to access the book.
**Additional Tips:** Each title on this website links to an external source where the eBook can be read or downloaded. Therefore, the number of formats and types of books varies greatly. This website is excellent as a reference tool and a starting point for finding educational works.

# 7. ePub Books

**Web address:** http://www.epubbooks.com

**Number of available books:** 520
**Categories:** Classics
**Prominent authors:** H.G. Wells, Agatha Christie, Charles Darwin, Aldous Huxley, James Joyce, and more
**Available formats:** Nook/Stanza (ePub)
**How to use:** Click 'Books', 'Authors', or 'Genres' at the top of the page to browse eBooks. Click a title to view its description. Click 'Download ePub' to get the free version of the book.
**Additional Tips:** Each eBook description provides a concise summary and eBook excerpt. In addition, each eBook description contains links to the eBook on other websites, such as Barnes and Noble and Kindle. If the eBook was also made into a motion picture, a link is provided.

# 8. Elegant Solutions Software and Publishing Company: eBooks for people who think

**Web address:** http://esspc-ebooks.com

**Number of available books:** 444
**Categories:** Modern Fiction, Classics, Children's, Romance, History, and many more
**Prominent authors:** H.B. Irving, Mark Twain, Henry James, Bram Stoker, The Brothers Grimm, and more
**Available formats:** Kindle/Mobi/Palm (PRC), Microsoft Reader (LIT)
**How to use:** Click 'New eBooks' or 'All titles' at the top of the page to browse books. Author, Title, and Genre searches are also available. Click the Microsoft Reader icon to download the LIT version of the book. Click the Mobipocket icon to download the PRC version of the eBook.
**Additional Tips:** Links are provided to download the Microsoft Reader as well as other useful software.

# 9. Feedbooks

**Web address**: http://www.feedbooks.com

**Number of available books:** 5300
**Categories:** Various, Mostly Short Stories and Science Fiction
**Prominent authors:** Francis Scott Fitzgerald, Edgar Allan Poe, Kurt Vonnegut, Isaac Asimov, Oscar Wilde, and more
**Available formats:** Nook/Stanza (ePub), Kindle/Mobi/Palm (PRC), and PDF
**How to use:** On the main page, click 'Public Domain' to view all free eBooks. Click a category on the left side of the page to browse eBooks. Click a title to view its description. Click a format to download the eBook.
**Additional Tips:** Feedbooks is an online community for bibliophiles. Click 'Register' at the top right of the page to create an account. With a registered account, books can be added to a favorites list, comments can be posted to eBook descriptions, and PDF's with custom settings can be downloaded.

# 10. Girlebooks - eBooks by female authors

**Web address:** http://girlebooks.com

**Number of available books:** 137
**Categories:** Female authors only
**Prominent authors:** Jane Austen, Louisa May Alcott, Virginia Woolf, Mary Shelley, Kate Chopin, and more
**Available formats:** Nook/Stanza (ePUB), Kindle/Mobi/Palm (PRC), Microsoft Reader (LIT), Plain Text (TXT), PDF
**How to use:** Click 'eBook Catalog' to view all eBooks. Click 'Select Category' to choose a genre. Click an eBook cover to view its description. Click a format to download it.
**Additional Tips:** Use the 'Also available at:' links to find the eBook on another website. Use the 'For Authors' link to submit your own work for consideration.

# 11. Project Gutenberg

**Web address:** http://www.gutenberg.org/wiki/Main_Page

**Number of available books:** 33,000
**Categories:** Classics
**Prominent authors:** Leo Tolstoy, Charles Dickens, Homer, Voltaire, Mary Shelley, and more
**Available formats:** Nook/Stanza (ePUB), Kindle/Mobi/Palm (PRC), HTML, Plucker (PDB), Plain Text (TXT), QiOO Mobile (QIOO)
**How to use:** Click 'Browse Catalog' and then click a letter under 'Authors' or 'Titles'. Click a language to view all related books. Click a title to view its description. Click the 'Download' tab to view all available formats. Click a format to download the eBook.
**Additional Tips:** Click 'Read this eBook online' to view the online HTML version of the book. Click 'Bookshelf' on the home page to view eBook suggestions for various genres. Click 'Partners, Affiliates, and Resources' on the home page to view links to additional Gutenberg sites and other eBook resources.

# 12. Internet Text Archive

**Web address:** http://www.archive.org/details/texts

**Number of available books:** 2,000,000
**Categories:** Various
**Prominent authors:** Various
**Available formats:** Various
**How to use:** This website is a reference tool for finding free eBooks on the internet. Use the Search field at the top of the page to find eBooks. Click the drop-down menu to select a database to search.
**Additional Tips:** Audio books are also available. Many links are provided to educational and other useful websites.

# 13. ManyBooks.net

**Web address:** http://manybooks.net

**Number of available books:** 29,000
**Categories:** Various
**Prominent authors:** Winston Churchill, T.S. Eliot, William Shakespeare, Karl Marx, Napoleon, and more
**Available formats:** Nook/Stanza (ePUB), Kindle/Mobi/Palm (PRC), HTML, PalmDOC (PDB), Plain Text (TXT), PDF, Rich Text (RTF), Sony Reader (LRF)
**How to use:** Click 'Authors', 'Titles', 'Genres', or 'Languages' to browse books. Click a title to view its description. Click the 'Download' drop-down menu to select a format. Click 'Download' to download the eBook. Some formats require registration.
**Additional Tips:** Registering with the website gives access to the Wishlist feature. Wikipedia and WorldCat links are provided to give more information about authors.

# 14. MobileRead Uploads

**Web address:** http://www.mobileread.com/forums/ebooks.php?order=desc&sort=dateline

**Number of available books:** 16,000
**Categories:** Action, Biography, Spiritual, Philosophy, Young Adult
**Prominent authors:** Daniel Defoe, H.G. Wells, Hans Christian Andersen, Agatha Christie, Bertrand Russell, and many more
**Available formats:** Nook/Stanza (ePUB), Kindle/Mobi/Palm (PRC), Sony Reader (LRF), eBookwise (IMP)
**How to use:** Click the 'Format' drop-down menu to select a format to display. Select 'ALL' to see all eBook formats. Click the 'Genre' drop-down menu to select an eBook category. Click 'Go' to view all related media. Click a title to view its description. Scroll down to the bottom of the page and click one of the attached files to download the eBook.
**Additional Tips:** MobileRead is an eBook community that contains blogs about many eBook topics. Links to other useful resources are also provided.

# 15. Munseys

**Web address:** http://www.munseys.com

**Number of available books:** 20,000
**Categories:** Various
**Prominent authors:** Francis Bacon, Lord Byron, O'Henry, Robert Sheckley, Ivan Turgenev, and more
**Available formats:** Nook/Stanza (ePUB), Kindle/Mobi/Palm (PRC), HTML, Plucker (PDB), PDF, Sony Reader (LRF), and Microsoft Reader
**How to use:** Scroll down on the home page to browse by category. Click the 'By' drop-down menu to select a search method and type in the related search term. Click a letter at the top of the search results to display all authors whose last name starts with that letter.
**Additional Tips:** Munseys uses tags, such as genres, titles, authors, and more. Tags allow readers to find books more easily. There is also a blog for sharing thoughts with fellow readers.

# 16. Planet eBook

**Web address:** http://www.planetebook.com

**Number of available books:** 82
**Categories:** Classics
**Prominent authors:** George Orwell, Jonathan Swift, John Milton, Franz Kafka, Herman Melville, and more
**Available formats:** PDF
**How to use:** All eBooks are listed on the home page. Click a title to view its description. Right-click '1-page version' (portrait) or '2-page version' (landscape) and click 'Save link as'. Click 'Save' to download the eBook.
**Additional Tips:** Blog and newsletter are available on this website.

# 17. Planet PDF

**Web address:** http://www.planetpdf.com/free_pdf_ebooks.asp

**Number of available books:** 60
**Categories:** Classics
**Prominent authors:** Charles Dickens, Aesop, James Joyce, Edgar Allan Poe, Robert Louis Stevenson, and more
**Available formats:** PDF
**How to use:** All available eBooks are listed on the home page. Click a title to view its description. Right-click a PDF icon and click 'Save link as'. Click 'Save' to download the eBook.
**Additional Tips:** This website provides tagged PDFs, which are optimized for eReaders, allowing better navigation on your Kindle.

# 18. Project Runeberg - Nordic Literature

**Web address:** http://runeberg.org

**Number of available books:** 1067
**Categories:** Nordic
**Prominent authors:** Various
**Available formats:** HTML
**How to use:** Click 'Catalog' at the top of the page to view all titles. Click a title to read it.
**Additional Tips:** The first eBook in the Catalog is a guide to learning the Norsk (Icelandic) language. This is necessary to be able to read the books.

# 19. Stanford Collection

**Web address:** http://collections.stanford.edu

**Number of available books:** Not applicable
**Categories:** Educational
**Prominent authors:** Various
**Available formats:** Various
**How to use:** Click a link to an external database to browse it.
**Additional Tips:** Not applicable

# 20. World Wide School

**Web address:** http://www.worldwideschool.org/library/catalogs/bysubject-top.html

**Categories:** Classics, Youth, History, Technology, Philosophy, Religion
**Prominent authors:** Various
**Available formats:** HTML
**How to use:** Click a genre to browse the related books. Click a title to read it. Click 'By Title' or 'By Author' at the top to sort the books accordingly.
**Additional Tips:** Not applicable

# Managing Your Media

## Table of Contents

## 1. Archiving an eBook

An eBook can be deleted from your Kindle and placed in archive. An archived eBook is retrievable by using the wireless connection. To archive an eBook, select an eBook at the home screen using the five-way controller and move the controller to the left. 'Remove from Device' appears, as shown in **Figure 1**. Push the five-way controller down. The eBook is archived.

*Warning: If 'Delete' appears instead of 'Remove from Device', the media will be deleted permanently. Usually, 'Delete' only appears when selecting a newspaper.*

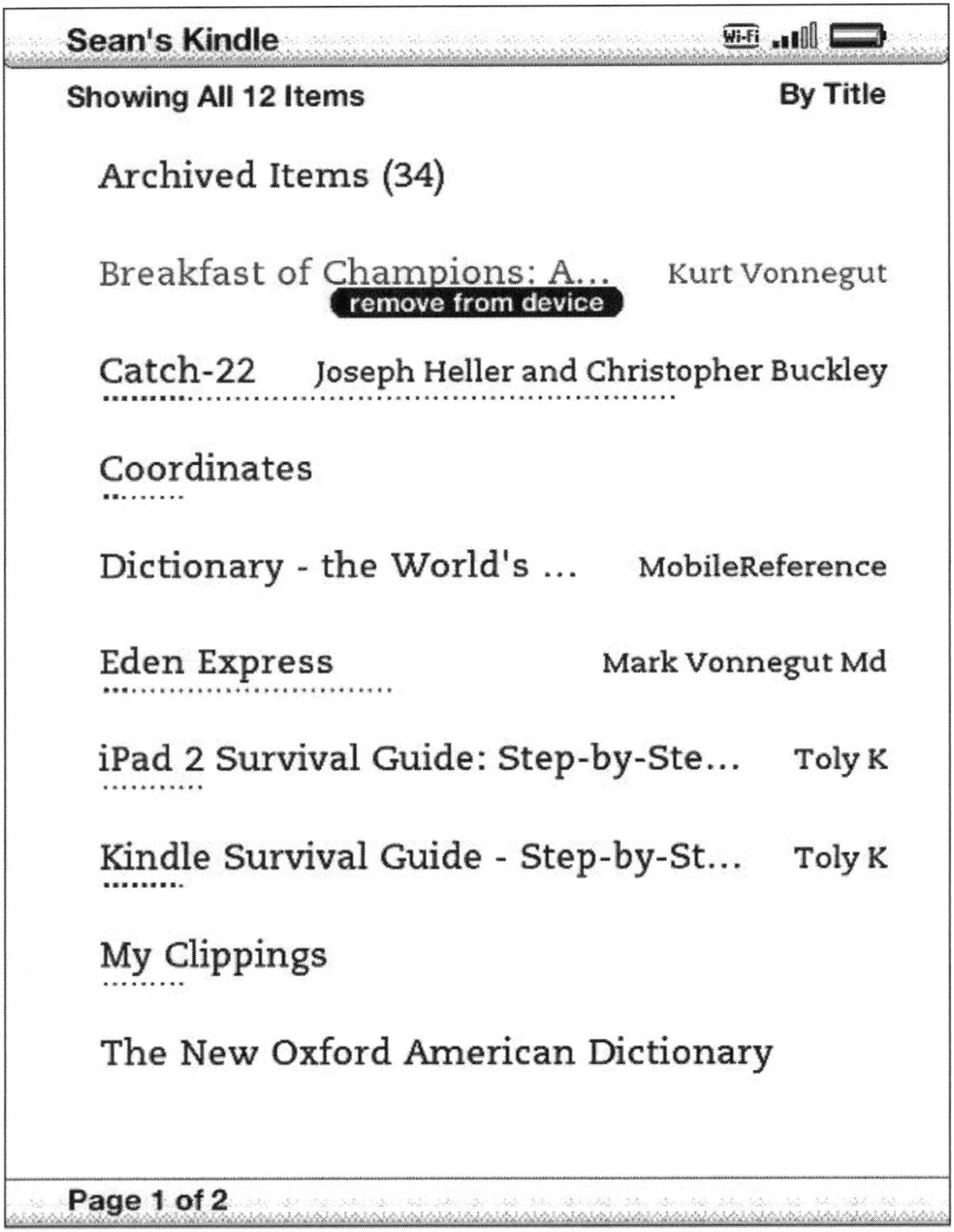

**Sean's Kindle** Wi-Fi

**Showing All 12 Items** **By Title**

Archived Items (34)

Breakfast of Champions: A...    Kurt Vonnegut
 **remove from device**

Catch-22    Joseph Heller and Christopher Buckley

Coordinates

Dictionary - the World's ...    MobileReference

Eden Express    Mark Vonnegut Md

iPad 2 Survival Guide: Step-by-Ste...    Toly K

Kindle Survival Guide - Step-by-St...    Toly K

My Clippings

The New Oxford American Dictionary

**Page 1 of 2**

*Figure 1: Archiving an eBook*

# 2. Restoring an Archived eBook

To restore an archived eBook, you must have Wireless turned on. To turn on Wireless, press the **Menu** button, select **Turn Wireless On** and push down on the five-way controller. To restore an archived eBook, select **Archived Items** at the Home screen using the five-way controller. Push the five-way controller down. The Archived Items screen appears. Select the eBook you wish to restore using the five-way controller. Push the five-way controller down. "Now downloading the selected item" appears and the eBook is restored.

*Note: The eBook automatically opens once the download is complete.*

# 3. Deleting a Periodical

In order to free up space on your Kindle, you may wish to delete a periodical issue. To delete a periodical:

***Warning: Once you delete a newspaper or magazine, it is permanently gone from your Kindle.***

1.  Select a periodical issue at the Home screen using the five-way controller. The media is selected.
2.  Move the five-way controller to the left. 'Delete' appears.
3.  Push the five-way controller down. The periodical issue is deleted.

# 4. Creating a Collection

Organize eBooks and other media into collections to enable you to locate them more easily. To create a collection:

1.  Press the **Menu** button at the Home screen. The Main menu appears, as shown in **Figure 2**.
2.  Select **Create New Collection** using the five-way controller. Push the controller down. The Collection Setup window appears, as shown in **Figure 3**.
3.  Type a name for the collection. The new name is entered.
4.  Select **Save** using the five-way controller. Push the controller down. The collection is created. The empty 'Travel Guides' collection is shown at the top of the list in **Figure 4**.

*Note: After adding eBooks to the collection, the number in parentheses will increase. Refer to the next section on page 63 to learn more.*

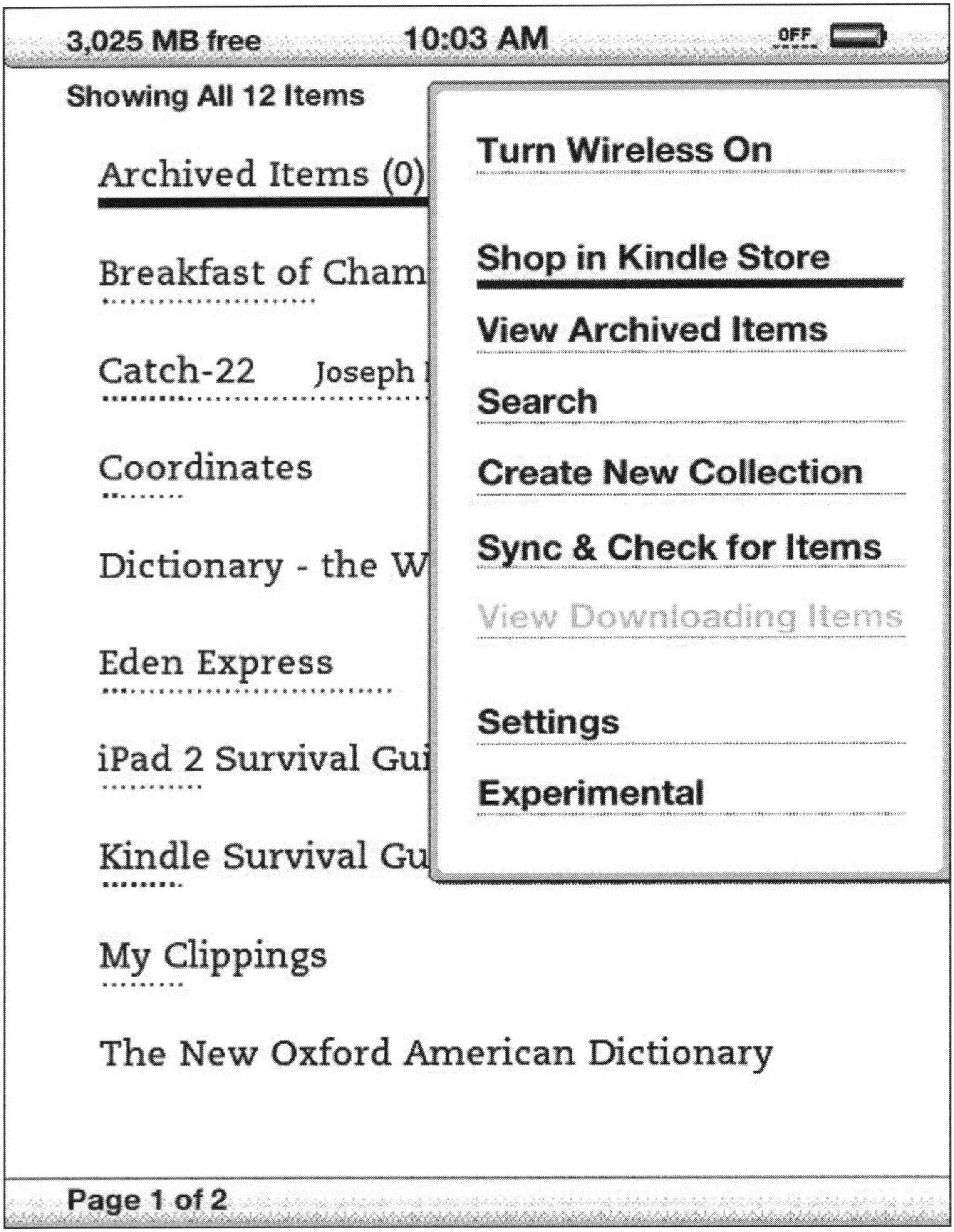

| 3,025 MB free | 10:03 AM | OFF ▭ |
|---|---|---|

**Showing All 12 Items**

Archived Items (0)

Breakfast of Cham

Catch-22   Joseph

Coordinates

Dictionary - the W

Eden Express

iPad 2 Survival Gui

Kindle Survival Gu

My Clippings

The New Oxford American Dictionary

**Turn Wireless On**

**Shop in Kindle Store**

**View Archived Items**

**Search**

**Create New Collection**

**Sync & Check for Items**

View Downloading Items

**Settings**

**Experimental**

**Page 1 of 2**

*Figure 2: Main menu*

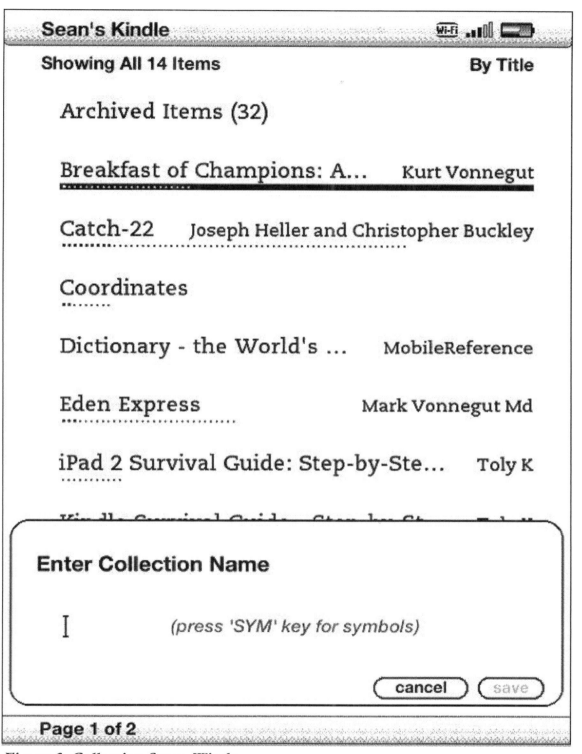

Figure 3: Collection Setup Window

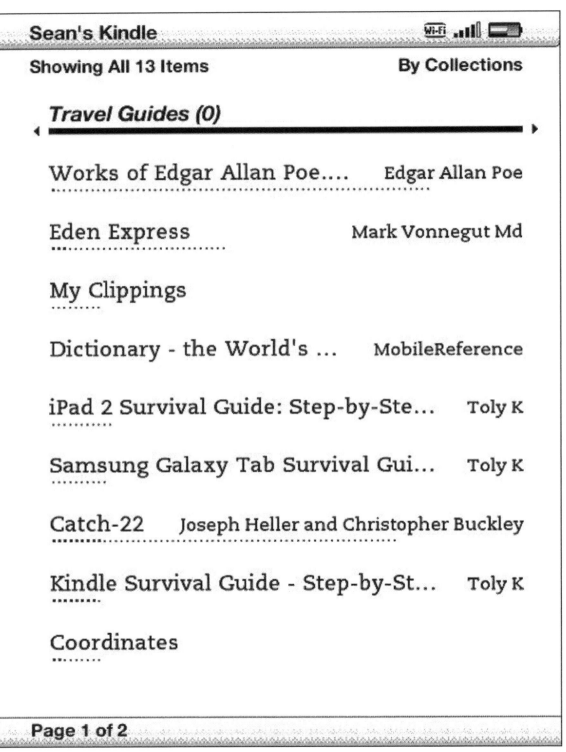

*Figure 4: Empty Travel Guides Collection*

# 5. Adding an eBook to a Collection

Once you have created a collection, you may add as many eBooks as you wish to it. To add eBooks or other media to a collection:

1. Select the eBook you would like to add to a collection using the five-way controller. Move the five-way controller to the right once. The Media-Specific menu appears, as shown in **Figure 5**.
2. Select **Add to Collection** using the five-way controller. Push the five-way controller down. A list of collections appears.
3. Choose a collection from the list using the five-way controller. If the list is empty, you must first create a collection. Refer to the previous section on page 59 to learn more.
4. Push the five-way controller down while the collection is underlined. A check mark appears and the eBook is immediately added to the collection, as shown in **Figure 6**.

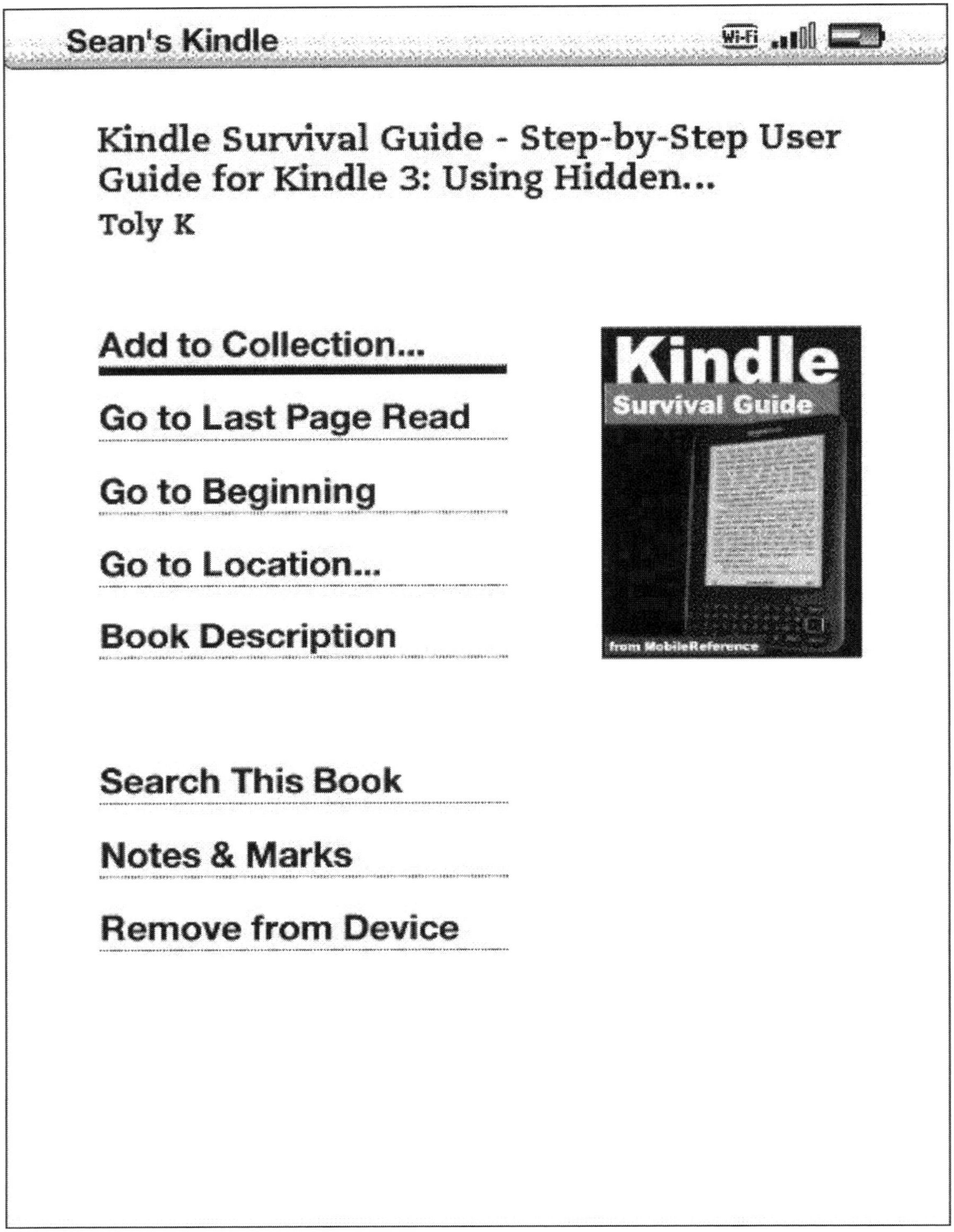

Sean's Kindle
Wi-Fi
Kindle Survival Guide - Step-by-Step User Guide for Kindle 3: Using Hidden...
Toly K
Add to Collection...
Go to Last Page Read
Go to Beginning
Go to Location...
Book Description
Search This Book
Notes & Marks
Remove from Device
Kindle
Survival Guide
from MobileReference

*Figure 5: Media-Specific Menu*

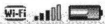

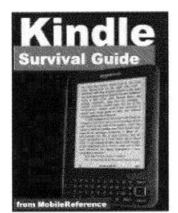

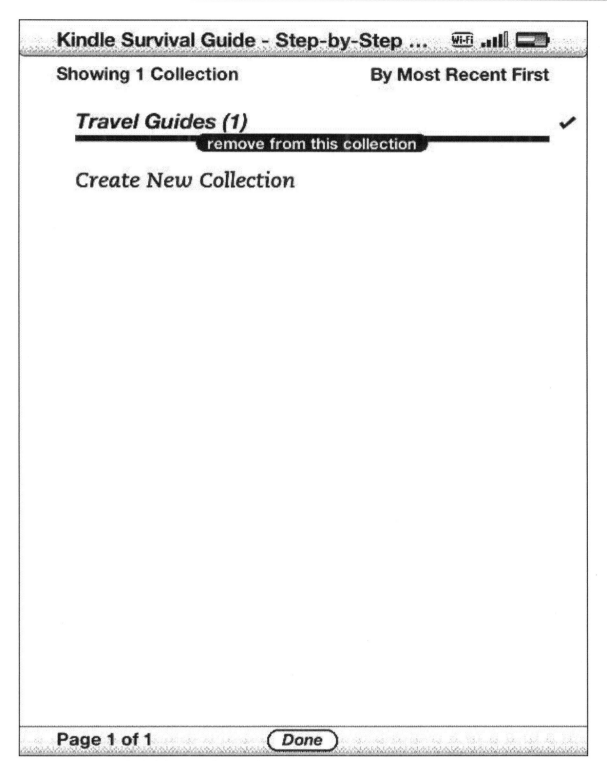

*Figure 6: eBook Added to Collection*

# 6. Removing an eBook from a Collection

You may remove an eBook from a collection if you would like to change the organization of your library. Removing an eBook from a collection does not delete it from your Kindle, and it can still be found in your library. To remove an eBook from a collection:

1.  Select a collection using the five-way controller. Move the five-way controller to the right once. The Media-Specific menu appears.
2.  Select **Add/Remove Items** using the five-way controller. Your library appears with check marks indicating the items that are in the collection, as shown in **Figure 7**.
3.  Select the eBook you wish to remove using the five-way controller. Push the five-way controller down. The media is removed from the collection.

*Figure 7: Kindle Library Indicating Titles Belonging to the Collection*

# 7. Viewing Popular Highlights

Some eBooks are marked up with popular highlights, which are passages that others have found to be the most interesting. To view popular highlights while reading:

1. Press the **Menu** button while reading. The eBook menu appears, as shown in **Figure 8**.
2. Select **View Popular Highlights** using the five-way controller. If it is grayed out, there are no popular highlights available for the eBook.
3. Push the five-way controller down. The Popular Highlights screen appears, as shown in **Figure 9**. The number to the right of each popular highlight represents the number of people who have highlighted the passage.
4. Select a highlight using your five-way controller. Push down the five-way controller. The Kindle navigates to the location of the highlight.
5. Press the **Back** button twice. The Kindle returns to the previous reading location.

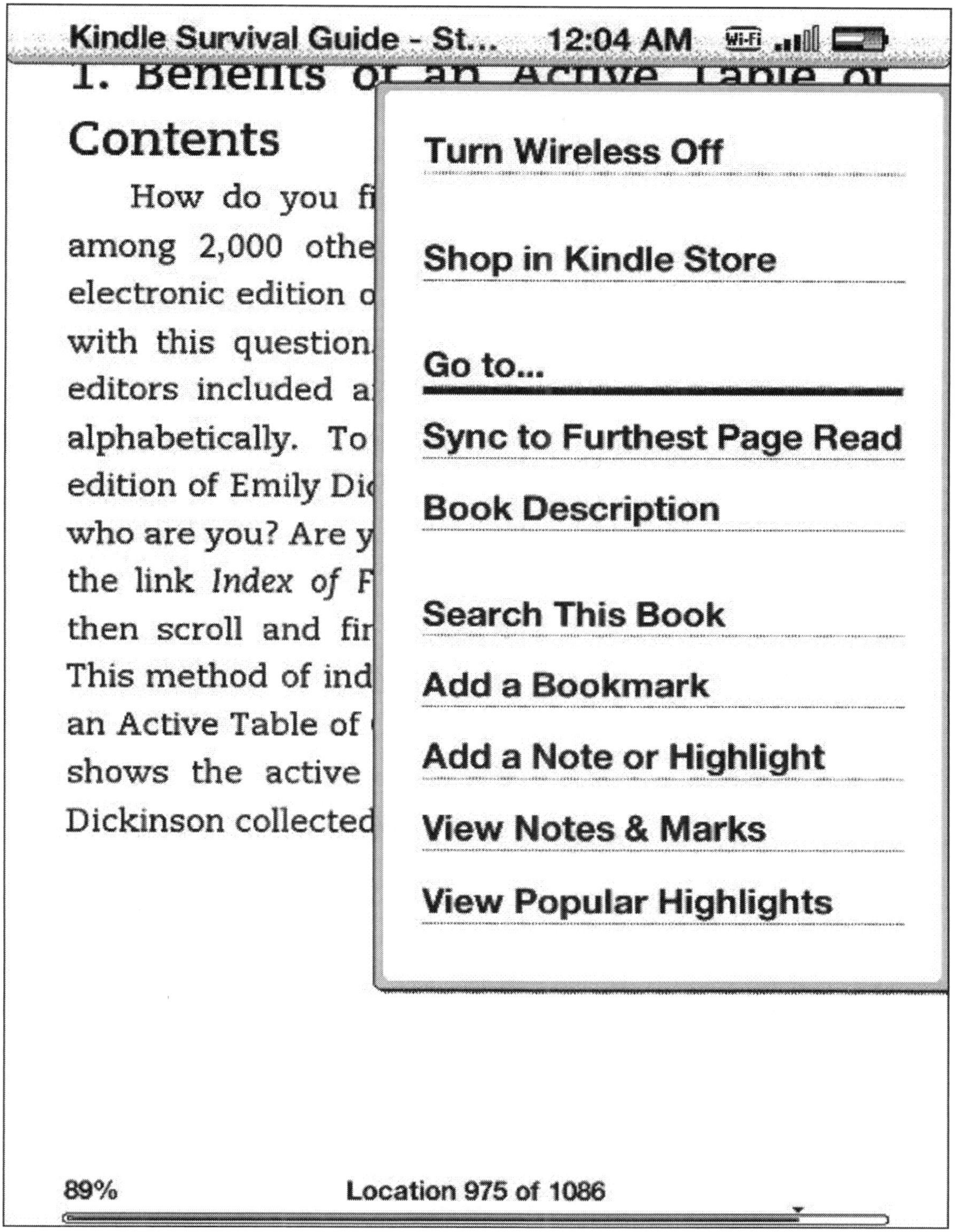

Kindle Survival Guide - St...     12:04 AM   Wi-Fi ..ıll ▭

# 1. Benefits of an Active Table of Contents

How do you fi
among 2,000 othe
electronic edition o
with this question.
editors included a
alphabetically. To
edition of Emily Dic
who are you? Are y
the link *Index of F*
then scroll and fir
This method of ind
an Active Table of
shows the active
Dickinson collected

**Turn Wireless Off**

**Shop in Kindle Store**

**Go to...**

**Sync to Furthest Page Read**

**Book Description**

**Search This Book**

**Add a Bookmark**

**Add a Note or Highlight**

**View Notes & Marks**

**View Popular Highlights**

89%                    Location 975 of 1086

*Figure 8: eBook Menu*

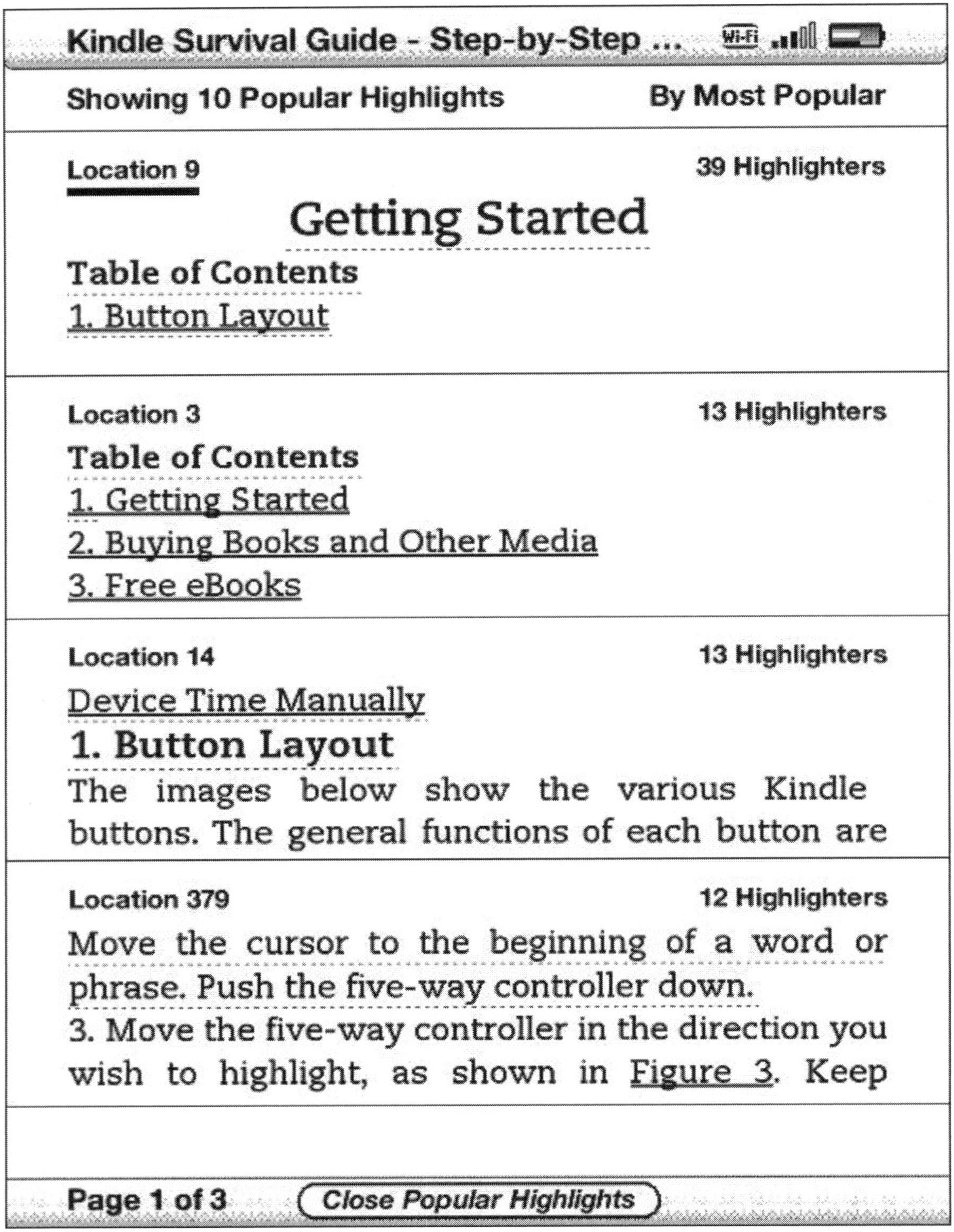

**Kindle Survival Guide - Step-by-Step ...**

Showing 10 Popular Highlights     By Most Popular

---

Location 9     39 Highlighters

# Getting Started

**Table of Contents**

1. Button Layout

---

Location 3     13 Highlighters

**Table of Contents**

1. Getting Started

2. Buying Books and Other Media

3. Free eBooks

---

Location 14     13 Highlighters

Device Time Manually

**1. Button Layout**

The images below show the various Kindle buttons. The general functions of each button are

---

Location 379     12 Highlighters

Move the cursor to the beginning of a word or phrase. Push the five-way controller down.

3. Move the five-way controller in the direction you wish to highlight, as shown in Figure 3. Keep

---

**Page 1 of 3**     ( *Close Popular Highlights* )

*Figure 9: Popular Highlights Screen*

# Reading eBooks

## Table of Contents

# 1. Navigating an eBook

The Kindle buttons and menus make it very easy to navigate an eBook. Use the following tips while reading:

**Navigating the Pages** - Press the **Next Page** and **Previous Page** buttons to navigate the pages of an eBook.

**Navigating Chapters and Articles** - Move the five-way controller to the left to go to the beginning of a chapter or article. Move the five-way controller to the left again to go to the previous chapter or article. Move the five-way controller to the right to go to the next chapter or article.

**Navigating to the Table of Contents** - Press the **Menu** button. The eBook menu appears, as shown in **Figure 1**. Select **Go to** using the five-way controller. Select **Table of Contents** and push the controller down again. The Kindle navigates to the Table of Contents.

**Navigating to the Beginning of an eBook** - Press the **Menu** button. The eBook menu appears. Select **Go to** using the five-way controller. Move the five-way controller down to select **beginning**. Push the controller down. The Kindle navigates to the beginning of the eBook.

**Navigating to a Specific Location** - Press the **Menu** button. The eBook menu appears. Select **Go to** using the five-way controller. Push the five-way controller down. A blank field appears at the bottom of the screen. Enter a number and press the return button. The Kindle navigates to the indicated location. Press the **SYM** button to access the numbers.

**Navigating to the Furthest Read Page** - You may navigate to the furthest page you have read on your device. Press the **Menu** button. The eBook menu appears. Select **Sync to Furthest Page Read** using the five-way controller. Push down the five-way controller. The Kindle navigates to the furthest read page.

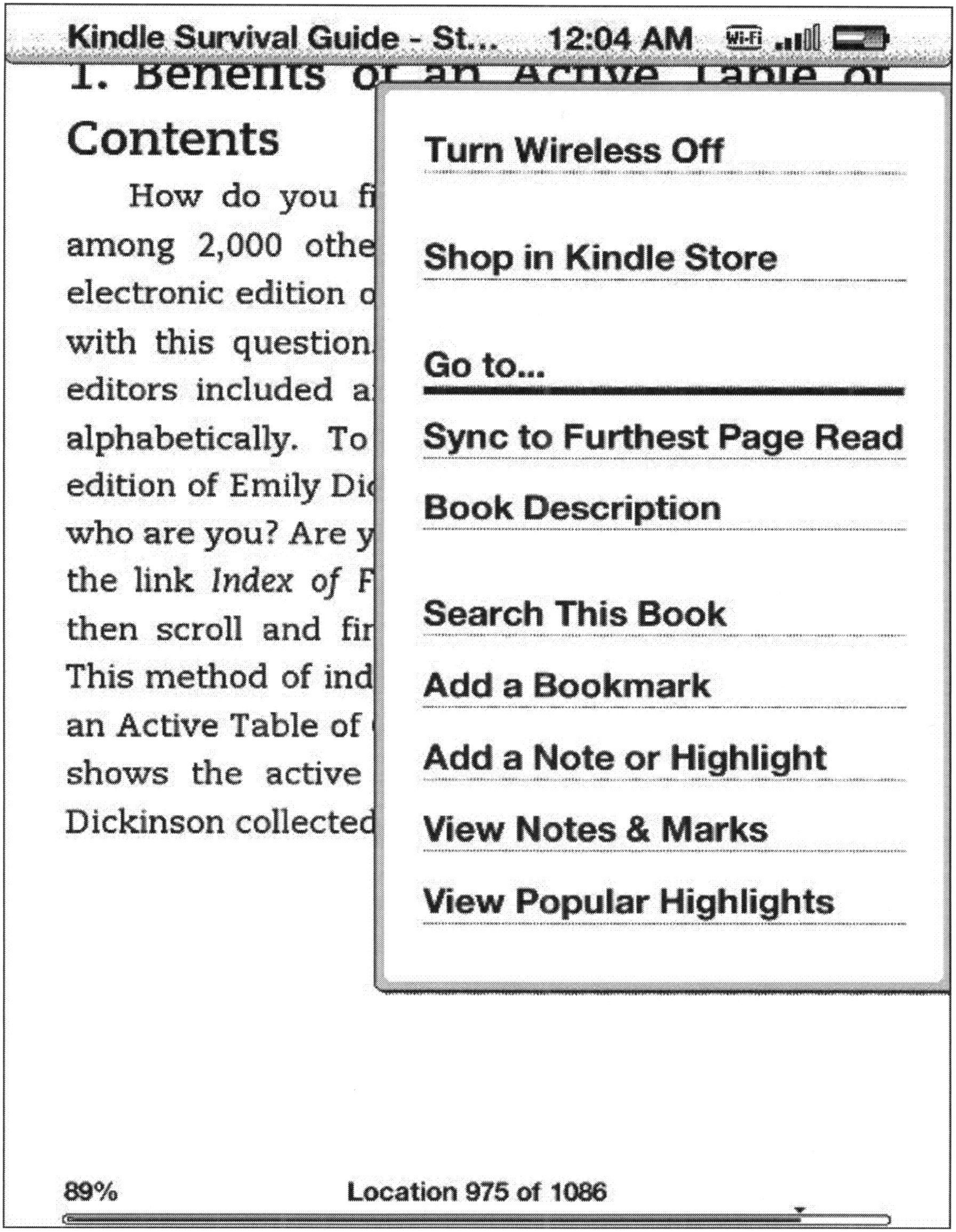

# 1. Benefits of an Active Table of Contents

How do you fi
among 2,000 othe
electronic edition o
with this question.
editors included a
alphabetically. To
edition of Emily Dic
who are you? Are y
the link *Index of F*
then scroll and fir
This method of ind
an Active Table of
shows the active
Dickinson collected

**Kindle Survival Guide - St...    12:04 AM    Wi-Fi**

**Turn Wireless Off**

**Shop in Kindle Store**

**Go to...**

**Sync to Furthest Page Read**

**Book Description**

**Search This Book**

**Add a Bookmark**

**Add a Note or Highlight**

**View Notes & Marks**

**View Popular Highlights**

89%          Location 975 of 1086

*Figure 1: eBook Menu*

## 2. Looking Up a Word in the Dictionary

While reading an eBook, magazine, or newspaper, use the built-in dictionary to look up word definitions. To look up a word:

1. Move the five-way controller in any direction. A cursor appears on the page.
2. Move the cursor to the beginning of a word using the five-way controller. A short definition appears at the top or bottom of the screen, as shown in **Figure 2**.
3. Press the return key (the rightmost key in the third row of the keyboard). The dictionary appears with the full definition, as shown in **Figure 3**.
4. Press the **Back** button. You are returned to the place in the eBook where you left off. To clear the cursor, press the **Back** button.

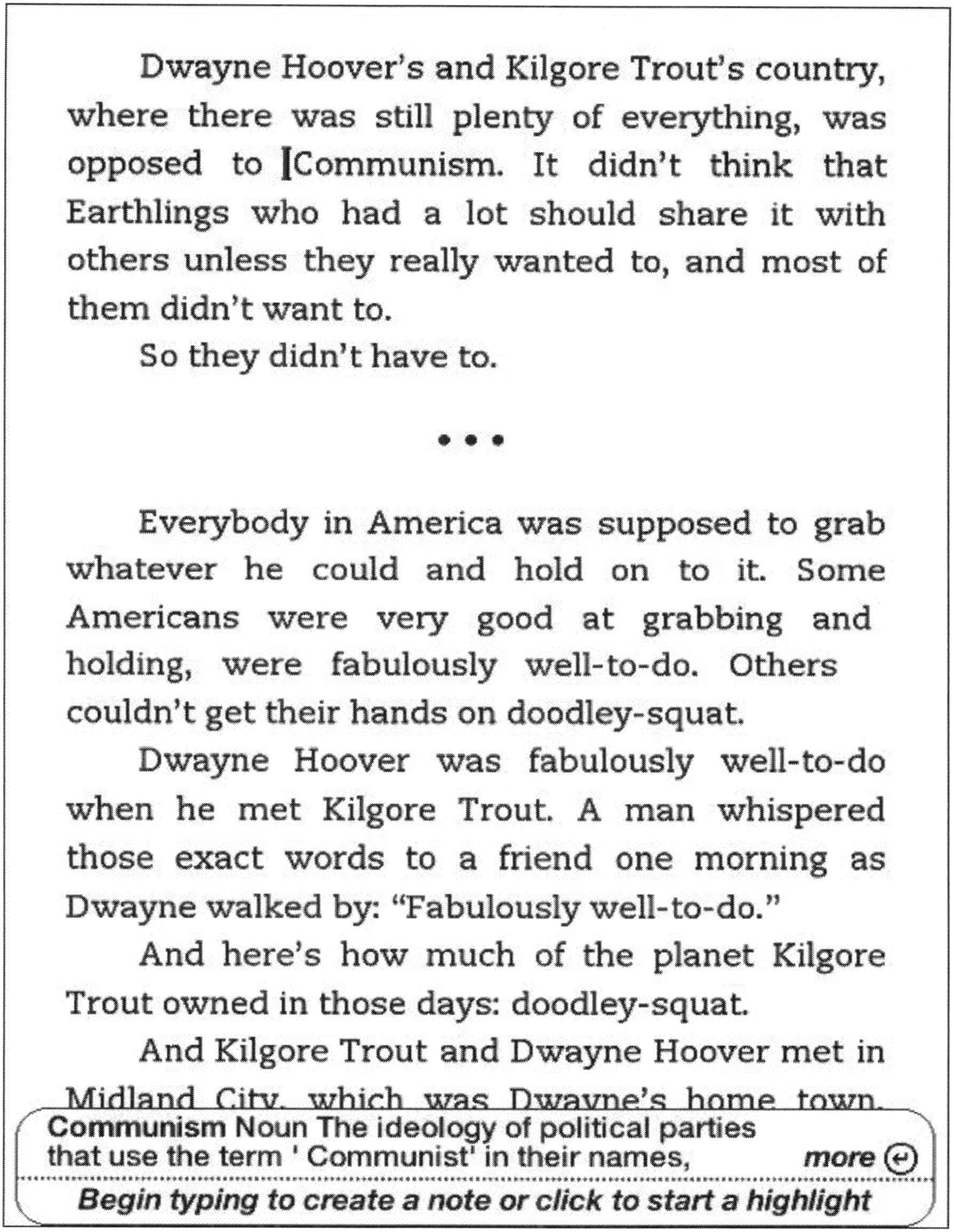

Dwayne Hoover's and Kilgore Trout's country, where there was still plenty of everything, was opposed to |Communism. It didn't think that Earthlings who had a lot should share it with others unless they really wanted to, and most of them didn't want to.

So they didn't have to.

• • •

Everybody in America was supposed to grab whatever he could and hold on to it. Some Americans were very good at grabbing and holding, were fabulously well-to-do. Others couldn't get their hands on doodley-squat.

Dwayne Hoover was fabulously well-to-do when he met Kilgore Trout. A man whispered those exact words to a friend one morning as Dwayne walked by: "Fabulously well-to-do."

And here's how much of the planet Kilgore Trout owned in those days: doodley-squat.

And Kilgore Trout and Dwayne Hoover met in Midland City, which was Dwayne's home town.

**Communism** Noun The ideology of political parties that use the term ' Communist' in their names,          *more* ⏎

*Begin typing to create a note or click to start a highlight*

*Figure 2: Quick Definition*

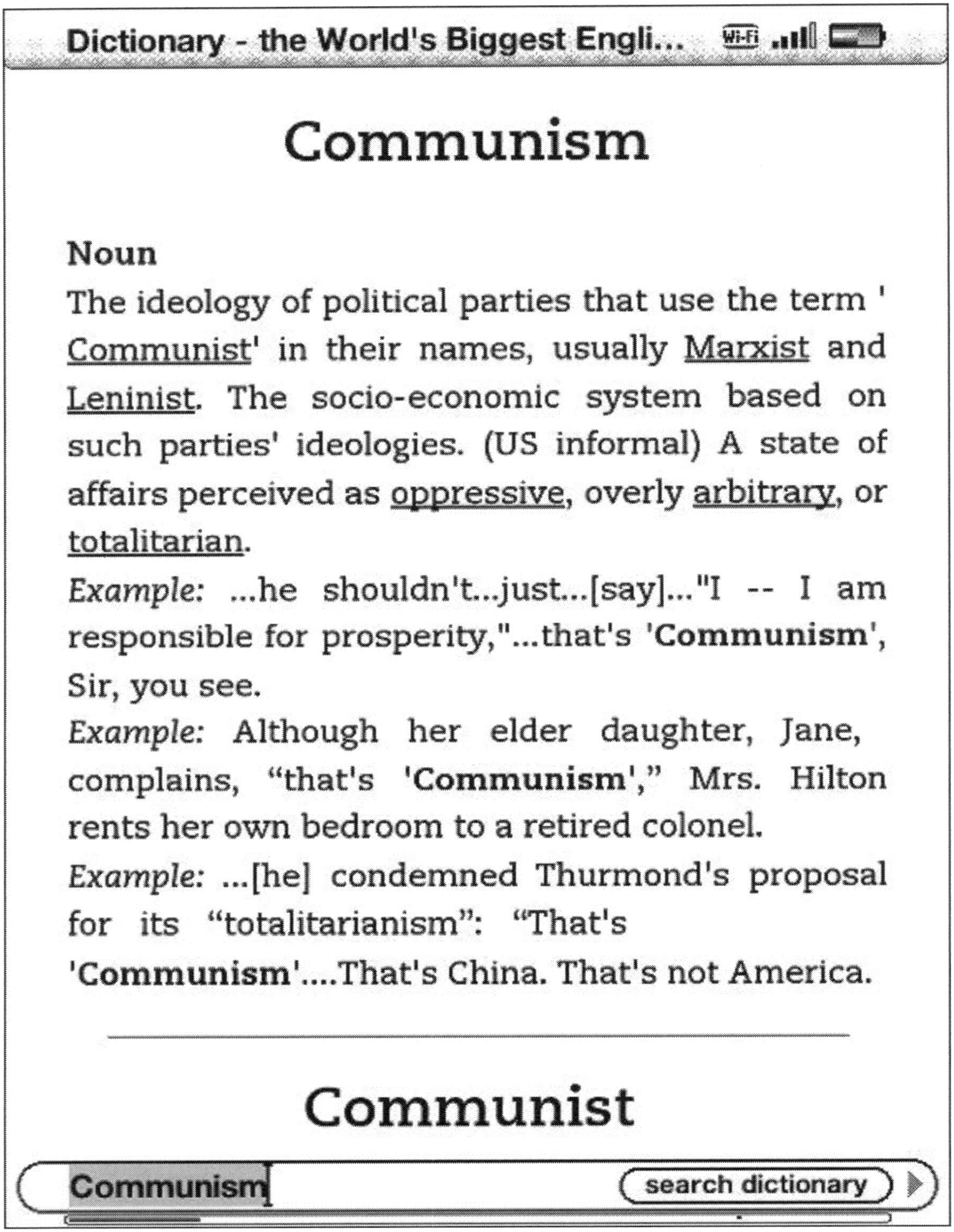

Dictionary - the World's Biggest Engli...

# Communism

**Noun**

The ideology of political parties that use the term ' Communist' in their names, usually Marxist and Leninist. The socio-economic system based on such parties' ideologies. (US informal) A state of affairs perceived as oppressive, overly arbitrary, or totalitarian.

*Example:* ...he shouldn't...just...[say]..."I -- I am responsible for prosperity,"...that's '**Communism**', Sir, you see.

*Example:* Although her elder daughter, Jane, complains, "that's '**Communism**'," Mrs. Hilton rents her own bedroom to a retired colonel.

*Example:* ...[he] condemned Thurmond's proposal for its "totalitarianism": "That's '**Communism**'....That's China. That's not America.

# Communist

Communism | search dictionary ▷

*Figure 3: Full Dictionary Definition*

# 3. Highlighting a Word or Phrase

While reading an eBook or periodical, words and phrases can be highlighted. To highlight a word or phrase:

1. Move the five-way controller up or down. The cursor appears at the top or bottom of the page.
2. Move the cursor to the beginning of a word or phrase. Push the five-way controller down. The highlighter is activated.
3. Move the five-way controller in any direction. The words in the eBook are highlighted, as shown in **Figure 4**. Keep moving the controller to highlight more words. To cancel a highlight, press the **Back** button.
4. Push the five-way controller down again. The highlight is saved.

*Note: To learn how to view your list of highlights, refer to "Viewing Your Notes, Highlights, and Bookmarks" on page 83.*

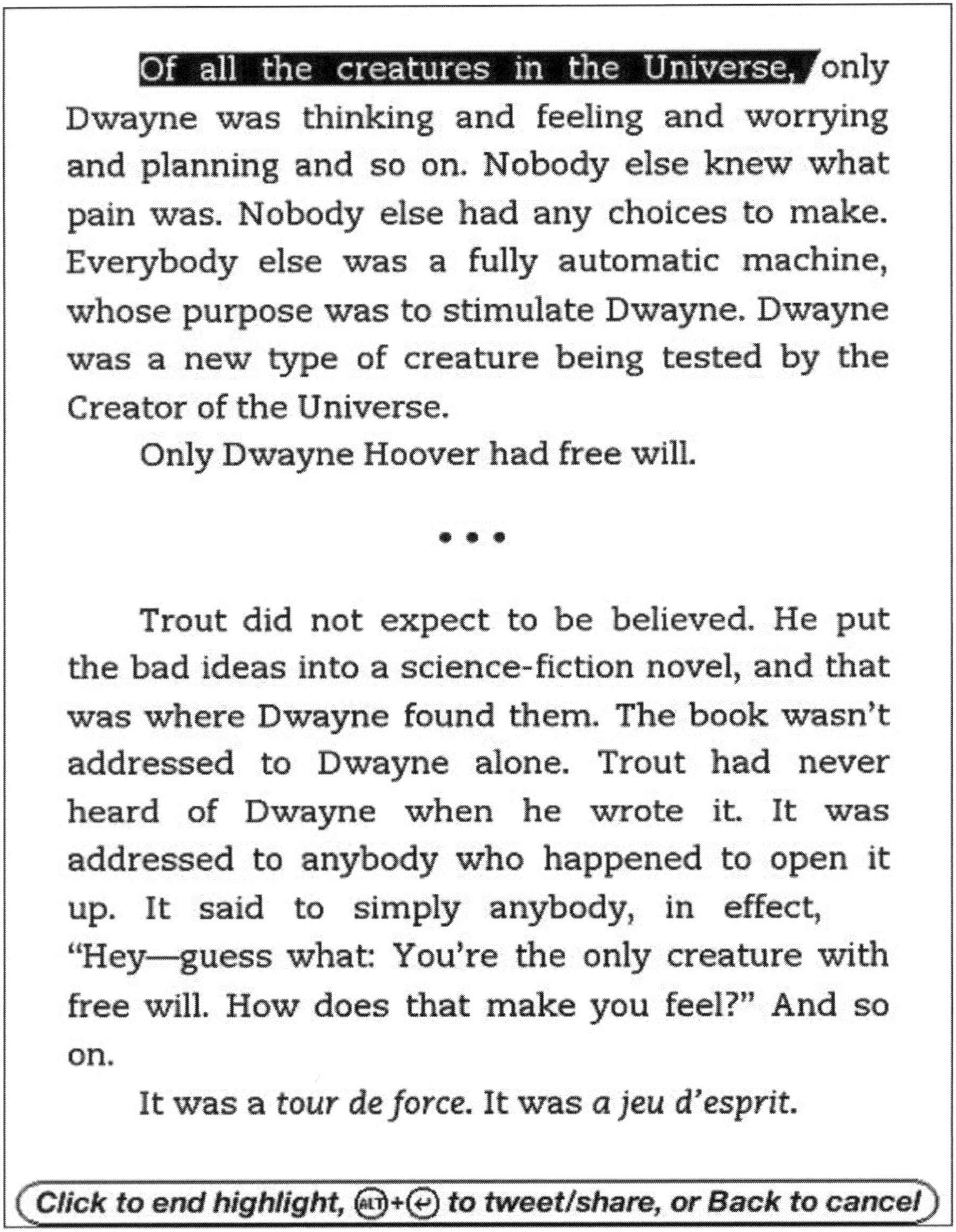

Of all the creatures in the Universe, only Dwayne was thinking and feeling and worrying and planning and so on. Nobody else knew what pain was. Nobody else had any choices to make. Everybody else was a fully automatic machine, whose purpose was to stimulate Dwayne. Dwayne was a new type of creature being tested by the Creator of the Universe.

Only Dwayne Hoover had free will.

• • •

Trout did not expect to be believed. He put the bad ideas into a science-fiction novel, and that was where Dwayne found them. The book wasn't addressed to Dwayne alone. Trout had never heard of Dwayne when he wrote it. It was addressed to anybody who happened to open it up. It said to simply anybody, in effect, "Hey—guess what: You're the only creature with free will. How does that make you feel?" And so on.

It was a *tour de force*. It was *a jeu d'esprit*.

Click to end highlight, (ALT)+(↵) to tweet/share, or Back to cancel

*Figure 4: Highlighted Words*

# 4. Making a Note

While reading an eBook or periodical, notes can be added at certain locations. To add a note:

1. Move the five-way controller up or down. The cursor appears at the top or bottom of the page.
2. Move the cursor to the place you would like to type your note. Start typing a note. The text appears in a window at the bottom of the screen, as shown in **Figure 5**.
3. Select **Save Note** using the five-way controller. Push the five-way controller down. A note is added and a number appears in the location of the cursor from step 1, representing the number of the note.

*Note: The numbers of the notes update automatically after adding or deleting notes. You may select the number with the cursor to display the note at any time. To learn how to view and navigate to your list of notes, refer to "Viewing Your Notes, Highlights, and Bookmarks" on page 83.*

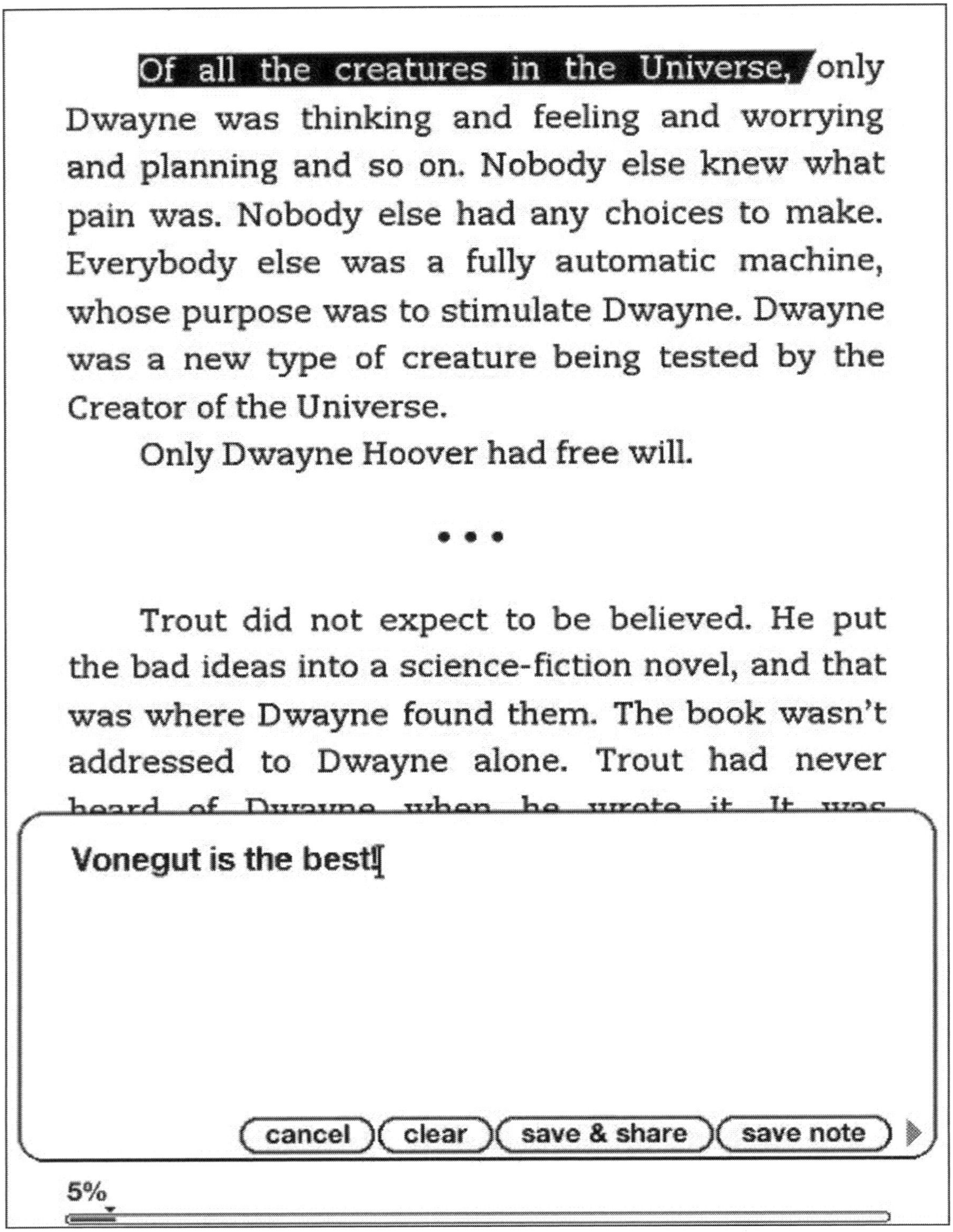

Of all the creatures in the Universe, only Dwayne was thinking and feeling and worrying and planning and so on. Nobody else knew what pain was. Nobody else had any choices to make. Everybody else was a fully automatic machine, whose purpose was to stimulate Dwayne. Dwayne was a new type of creature being tested by the Creator of the Universe.

Only Dwayne Hoover had free will.

• • •

Trout did not expect to be believed. He put the bad ideas into a science-fiction novel, and that was where Dwayne found them. The book wasn't addressed to Dwayne alone. Trout had never heard of Dwayne when he wrote it. It was

**Vonegut is the best**|

( cancel )( clear )( save & share )( save note ) ▶

5%

*Figure 5: Typing a Note*

# 5. Adding a Bookmark

While reading an eBook or periodical, the media can be bookmarked at certain locations. To add a bookmark, press the **Menu** button. The eBook Menu appears. Select **Add a Bookmark** using the five-way controller. Push the five-way controller down. The top right corner of the page is folded down to indicate that the page is bookmarked, as shown in **Figure 6**.

*Note: To learn how to view your list of bookmarks, refer to the next section, "Viewing Your Notes, Highlights, and Bookmarks on page 83.*

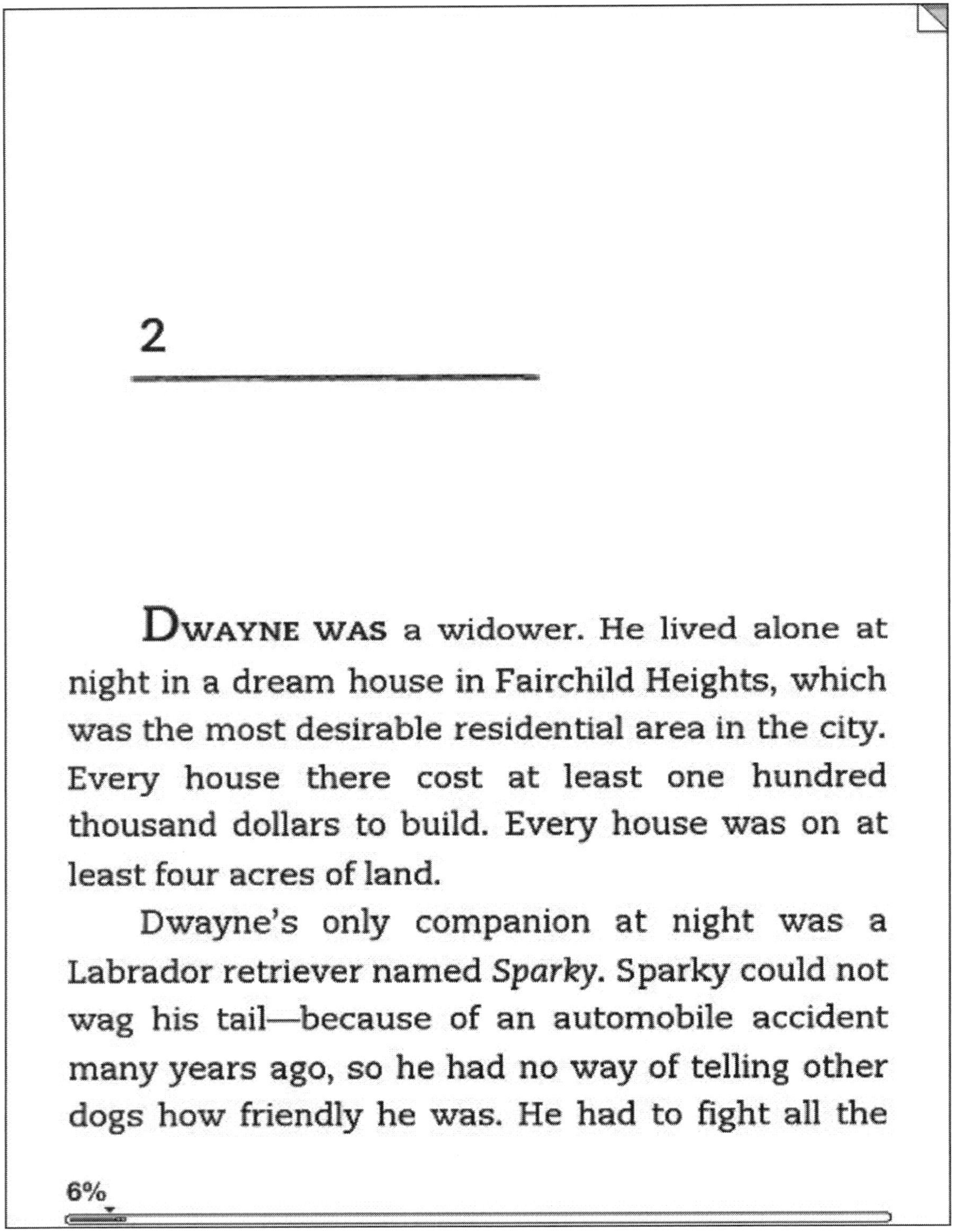

## 2

Dwayne was a widower. He lived alone at night in a dream house in Fairchild Heights, which was the most desirable residential area in the city. Every house there cost at least one hundred thousand dollars to build. Every house was on at least four acres of land.

Dwayne's only companion at night was a Labrador retriever named *Sparky*. Sparky could not wag his tail—because of an automobile accident many years ago, so he had no way of telling other dogs how friendly he was. He had to fight all the

6%

*Figure 6: Bookmark Added*

# 6. Viewing Your Notes, Highlights, and Bookmarks

While reading an eBook or periodical, you may view a list of all of your bookmarks, notes, and highlights and navigate to each directly. To view your list of bookmarks, notes, and highlights:

1.  Press the **Menu** button. The eBook menu appears.
2.  Select **View Notes & Marks** using the five-way controller. Push the five-way controller down. The list of notes, bookmarks, and highlights appears, as shown in **Figure 7**.
3.  Select a highlight, note, or bookmark using the five-way controller. Push the five-way controller down. The Kindle navigates to the selected location in the eBook.
4.  Press the **Back** button. The list of notes and highlights appears.
5.  Press the **Back** button again. The Kindle returns to the location where you left off.

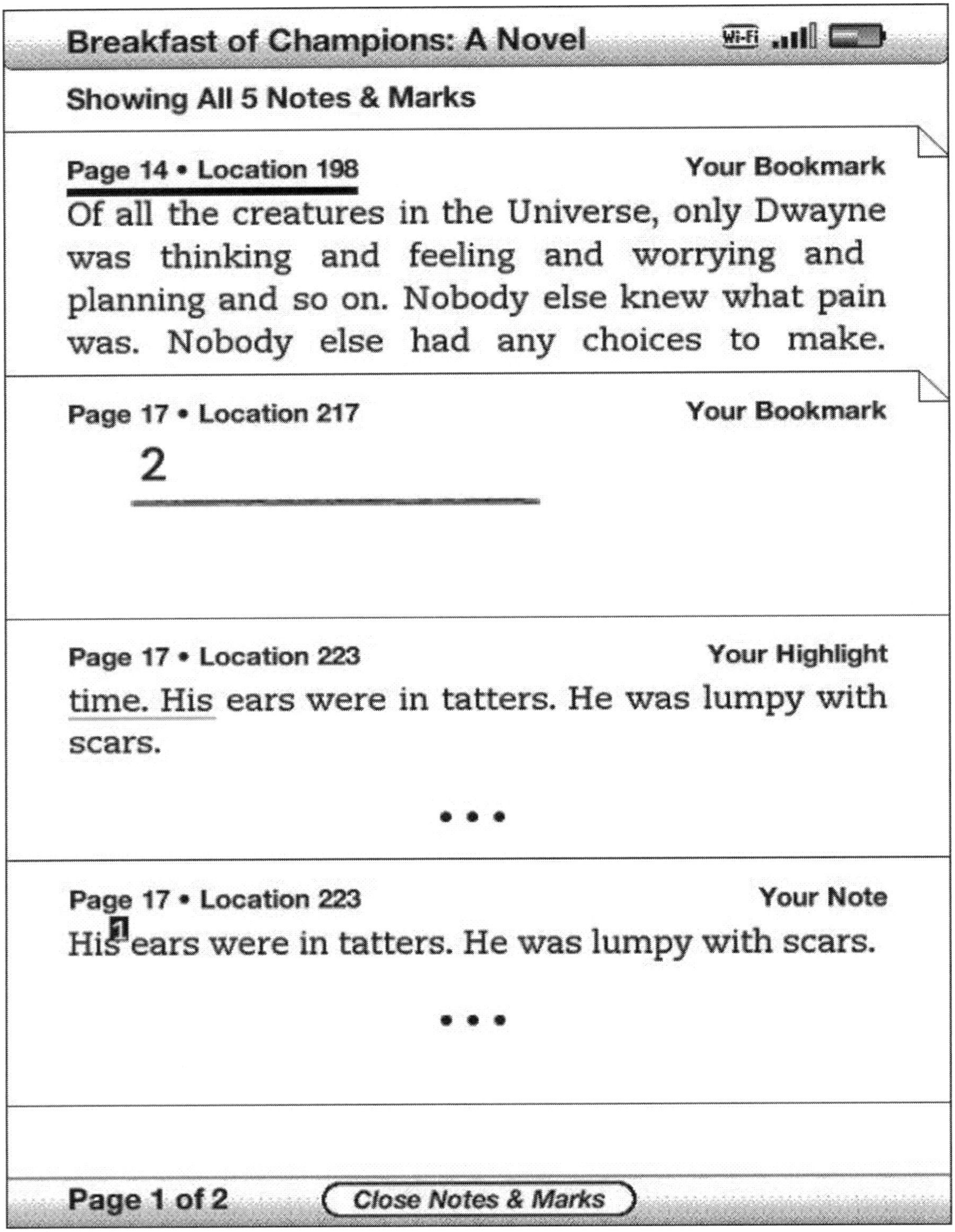

**Breakfast of Champions: A Novel**   Wi-Fi ..ıll ▭

**Showing All 5 Notes & Marks**

**Page 14 • Location 198**                     **Your Bookmark**

Of all the creatures in the Universe, only Dwayne
was thinking and feeling and worrying and
planning and so on. Nobody else knew what pain
was. Nobody else had any choices to make.

**Page 17 • Location 217**                     **Your Bookmark**

2

**Page 17 • Location 223**                     **Your Highlight**

time. His ears were in tatters. He was lumpy with
scars.

• • •

**Page 17 • Location 223**                     **Your Note**

His ears were in tatters. He was lumpy with scars.

• • •

**Page 1 of 2**          ( *Close Notes & Marks* )

*Figure 7: List of Bookmarks, Highlights, and Notes*

# 7. Changing the Font Size

While reading an eBook, the size of the text can be changed. To change the font size:

1. Press the **Aa** button, located in the bottom row of the Kindle. The Text menu appears, as shown in **Figure 8**.
2. Move the five-way controller to the left or right. The size of the text decreases or increases accordingly. The font size in the eBook is adjusted to preview the result.
3. Press the **Aa** button again. The font size is updated.

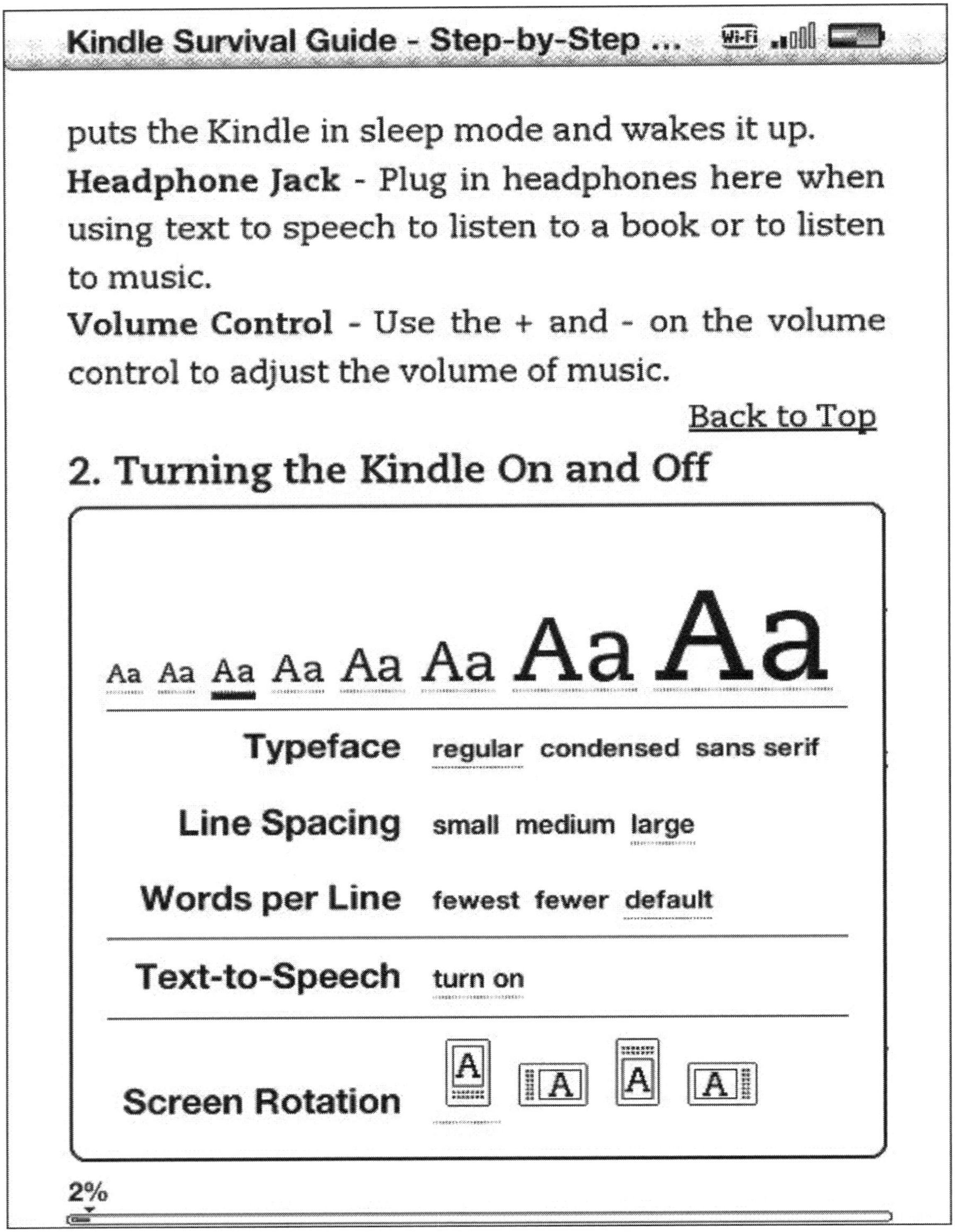

Kindle Survival Guide - Step-by-Step ...
Wi-Fi
puts the Kindle in sleep mode and wakes it up.
Headphone Jack - Plug in headphones here when using text to speech to listen to a book or to listen to music.
Volume Control - Use the + and - on the volume control to adjust the volume of music.
Back to Top
2. Turning the Kindle On and Off
Aa Aa Aa Aa Aa Aa Aa Aa
Typeface
regular condensed sans serif
Line Spacing
small medium large
Words per Line
fewest fewer default
Text-to-Speech
turn on
Screen Rotation
A A A A
2%

*Figure 8: Text Menu*

## 8. Changing the Font Type

While reading an eBook, the type of font displayed can be changed. To change the font type:

1. Press the **Aa** button, located in the bottom row of the Kindle. The Text menu appears.
2. Select **regular** next to 'Typeface' using the five-way controller. Move the five-way controller to the right or left to change the font. The font is adjusted in the eBook to preview the result.
3. Press the **Aa** button again. The font is updated.

## 9. Changing the Line Spacing

While reading an eBook, the amount of space between each line can be altered for easier reading. To change the line spacing:

1. Press the **Aa** button, located in the bottom row of the Kindle. The Text menu appears.
2. Select **large** next to 'Line Spacing' using the five-way controller. Move the five-way controller to the right or left to change the line spacing. The line spacing is adjusted in the eBook to preview the result.
3. Press the **Aa** button again. The line spacing is updated.

## 10. Changing the Number of Words per Line

While reading an eBook, you may change the number of words that appear on one line, which changes the size of the left and right margins. To change the number of words per line:

1. Press the **Aa** button, located in the bottom row of the Kindle. The Text menu appears.
2. Move the five-way controller down once. The current number of words per line (fewest, fewer, default) is selected.
3. Move the five-way controller to the left or right. The number of words per line decreases or increases accordingly. The words per line are adjusted in the eBook to show the preview of the result.
4. Press the **Aa** button again. The number of words per line is updated.

# 11. Turning Text-to-Speech On and Off

Some eBooks have the capability to use the Kindle's Text-to-Speech feature, which reads the eBook aloud. If the eBook does not have this capability, the feature will be grayed out in the Text menu. To turn Text-to-Speech on or off:

1. Press the **Aa** button, located in the bottom row of the Kindle. The Text menu appears.
2. Select **Turn on** next to 'Text-to-Speech' using the five-way controller. Push the controller down. The speaker begins to read at the top of the current page or wherever Text-to-Speech last left off.
3. Press the **Aa** button again. Select **Turn Off** next to 'Text-to-Speech' using the five-way controller.
4. Push the five-way controller down. Text-to-Speech is turned off.

*Note: You may also pause Text-to-Speech by selecting* **Pause** *using the five-way controller. Push the five-way controller down to pause Text-to-Speech. Text-to-Speech is automatically turned off after exiting an eBook using the Home button.*

# 12. Changing the Speech Rate

While Text-to-Speech is turned on, the speed of the reading voice can be changed. To change the speech rate:

1. Press the **Aa** button, located in the bottom row of the Kindle. The Text-to-Speech menu appears, as shown in **Figure 9**.
2. Select **slower**, **default**, or **faster** next to 'Speech Rate' using the five-way controller.
3. Move the five-way controller to the left or right. The speech rate decreases or increases accordingly.
4. Push the five-way controller down. The Text menu disappears and the speech rate is set to the selected speed.

puts the Kindle in sleep mode and wakes it up.

**Headphone Jack** - Plug in headphones here when using text to speech to listen to a book or to listen to music.

**Volume Control** - Use the + and - on the volume

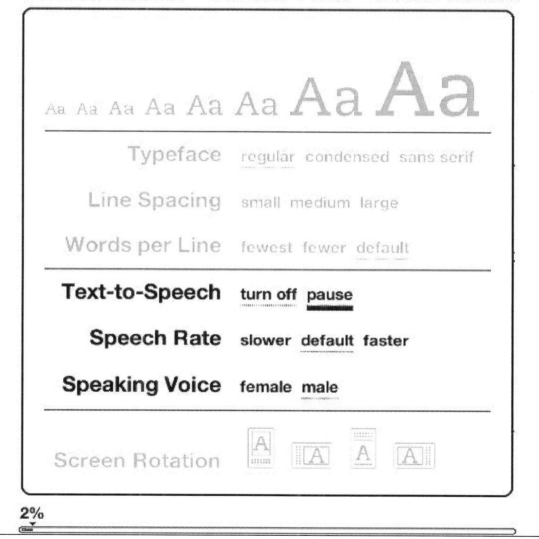

*Figure 9: Text-to-Speech Menu*

# 13. Changing the Speaking Voice

While Text-to-Speech is turned on, you may set the speaker to either a male or a female voice. To change the speaking voice:

1. Press the **Aa** button, located in the bottom row of the Kindle. The Text-to-Speech menu appears.
2. Select **female** or **male** next to 'Speaking Voice' using the five-way controller.
3. Move the five-way controller to the left or right to select the desired voice. Push the five-way controller down to confirm your selection. The speaking voice is changed.

# 14. Changing the Screen Orientation

While reading an eBook, the screen can be rotated. To change the screen orientation, press the **Aa** button, located in the bottom row of the Kindle. The Text menu appears. Select one of the Kindle icons using the five-way controller. The orientation is represented by the large 'A' in each icon. Push the five-way controller down to confirm the selection. The screen orientation is changed.

*Note: After rotating the screen, the five-way controller works in relation to the new orientation. For example, if you rotated the screen to the right, what was 'right' on the five-way controller is now 'down'.*

# 15. Searching an eBook

You may search an eBook for a particular word or phrase. To search an eBook:

1. While reading an eBook, make sure there is no cursor on the page (this results from moving the five-way controller while reading). If there is a cursor on the page, press the **Back** button to make it disappear.
2. Type the search word or phrase and push down the five-way controller. A list of all locations containing the word or phrase appears, as shown in **Figure 10**.
3. Use the **Next Page** and **Previous Page** buttons to navigate the list. The number of pages is shown at the bottom left corner of the screen.
4. To navigate to the location of a search result, move the five-way controller up or down to select that result. Push the five-way controller down. The Kindle opens the selected page in the eBook.

*Note: If you start typing while there is a cursor on the page, a note will be added and a search will not be performed.*

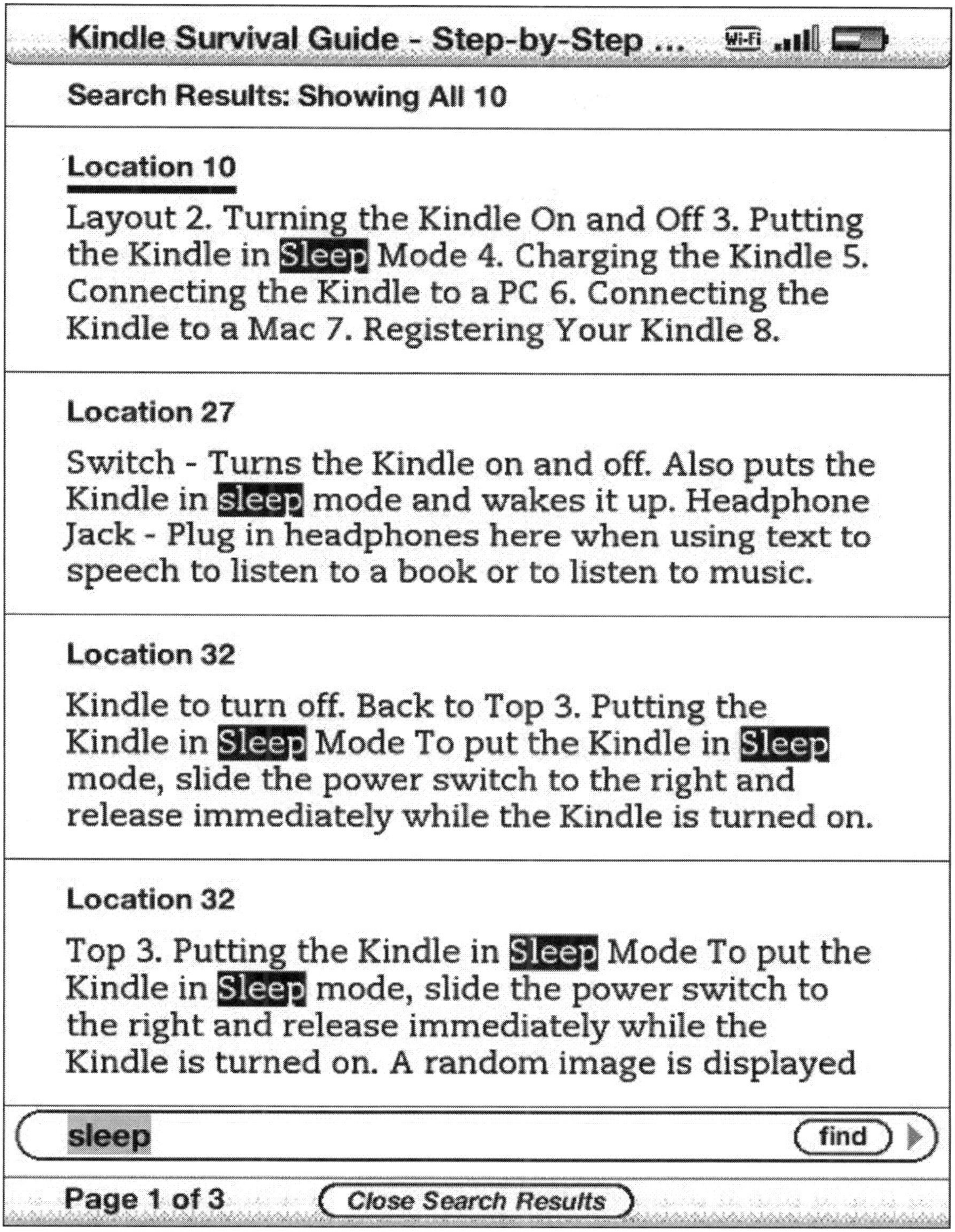

**Kindle Survival Guide - Step-by-Step ...** 📶 ▂▃▅ 🔋

**Search Results: Showing All 10**

### Location 10

Layout 2. Turning the Kindle On and Off 3. Putting the Kindle in `Sleep` Mode 4. Charging the Kindle 5. Connecting the Kindle to a PC 6. Connecting the Kindle to a Mac 7. Registering Your Kindle 8.

### Location 27

Switch - Turns the Kindle on and off. Also puts the Kindle in `sleep` mode and wakes it up. Headphone Jack - Plug in headphones here when using text to speech to listen to a book or to listen to music.

### Location 32

Kindle to turn off. Back to Top 3. Putting the Kindle in `Sleep` Mode To put the Kindle in `Sleep` mode, slide the power switch to the right and release immediately while the Kindle is turned on.

### Location 32

Top 3. Putting the Kindle in `Sleep` Mode To put the Kindle in `Sleep` mode, slide the power switch to the right and release immediately while the Kindle is turned on. A random image is displayed

`sleep`                                                      ( find ) ▶

**Page 1 of 3**         ( *Close Search Results* )

*Figure 10: Search Results*

# 16. Viewing an eBook Description

To read a brief description of an eBook you own, Wireless must be turned on. Refer to "Turning On Wireless" on page 105 to learn more. To read an eBook description:

1. Select an eBook at the Home screen using the five-way controller. Move the five-way controller to the right. The Media-specific menu appears, as shown in **Figure 11**.
2. Select **Book Description** using the five-way controller. Push down the controller. The eBook description appears.
3. Select **More** using the five-way controller. Push down the five-way controller. The full description appears.

**Sean's Kindle**

## Kindle Survival Guide - Step-by-Step User Guide for Kindle 3: Using Hidden...
Toly K

**Add to Collection...**

**Go to Last Page Read**

**Go to Beginning**

**Go to Location...**

**Book Description**

**Search This Book**

**Notes & Marks**

**Remove from Device**

*Figure 11: Media-Specific Menu*

# Surfing the Web

## Table of Contents

## 1. Opening the Web Browser

The Kindle has a built-in web browser. You must have wireless turned on to use the browser. To learn how to turn on wireless, refer to "Turning on Wireless" on page 104. To open the web browser:

1. Press the **Menu** button at the Home screen. The Main menu appears, as shown in **Figure 1**.
2. Select **Experimental** using the five-way controller and push it down. The Experimental Menu appears, as shown in **Figure 2**.
3. Select **Launch Browser** using the five-way controller and push down. The web browser opens and the most recently viewed page appears, as shown in **Figure 3**.

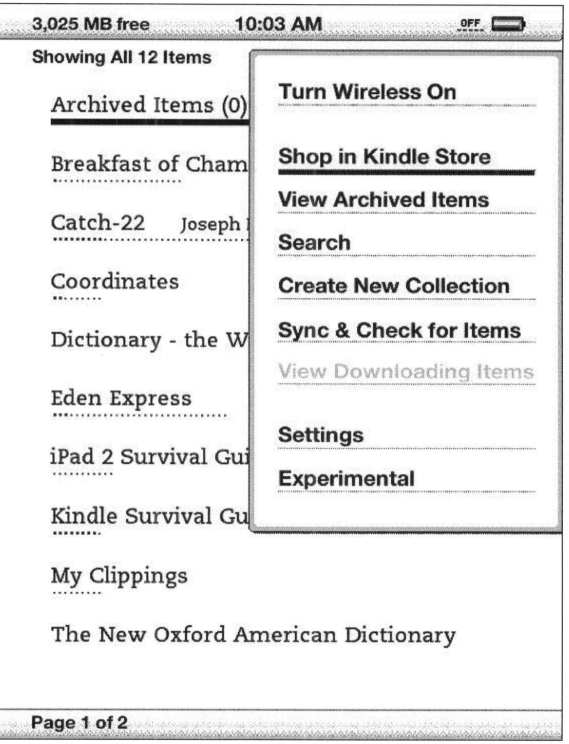

*Figure 1: Main Menu*

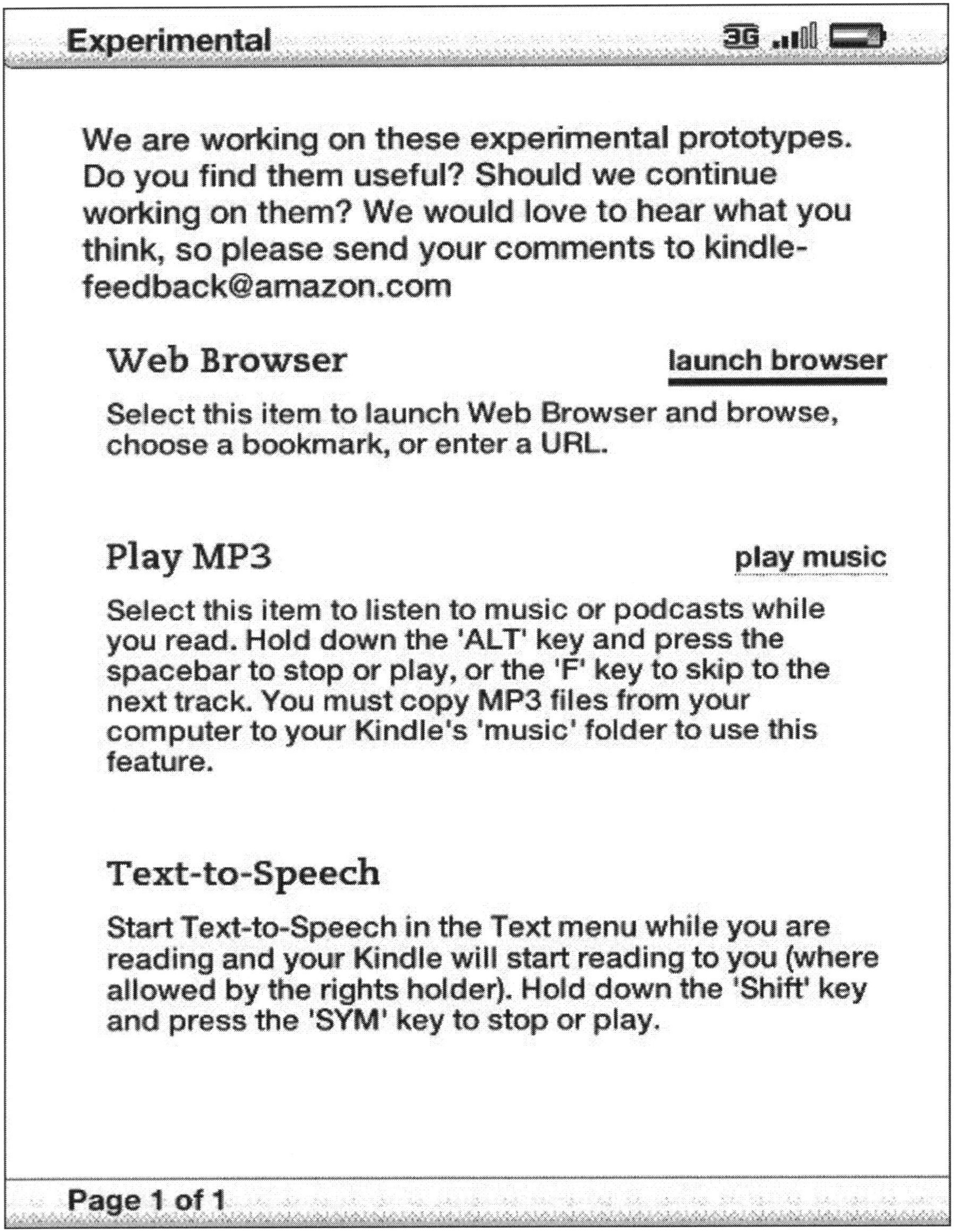

**Experimental**          3G .ıll 🔋

We are working on these experimental prototypes. Do you find them useful? Should we continue working on them? We would love to hear what you think, so please send your comments to kindle-feedback@amazon.com

## Web Browser                     launch browser

Select this item to launch Web Browser and browse, choose a bookmark, or enter a URL.

## Play MP3                          play music

Select this item to listen to music or podcasts while you read. Hold down the 'ALT' key and press the spacebar to stop or play, or the 'F' key to skip to the next track. You must copy MP3 files from your computer to your Kindle's 'music' folder to use this feature.

## Text-to-Speech

Start Text-to-Speech in the Text menu while you are reading and your Kindle will start reading to you (where allowed by the rights holder). Hold down the 'Shift' key and press the 'SYM' key to stop or play.

Page 1 of 1

*Figure 2: Experimental Menu*

*Figure 3: Open Web Browser*

## 2. Navigating to a Website

To navigate to a website, use the Kindle web browser. Refer to the previous section, "Opening the Web Browser" on page 94, to learn more. To go to a specific website:

1. Press the **Menu** button while in the browser. The Browser menu appears, as shown in **Figure 4**.
2. Select **Enter URL** using the five-way controller. Push the five-way controller down. The address at the top of the page is selected. If 'Enter URL' is grayed out, the address bar is already selected.
3. Type the address of the website you wish to visit. Push down the five-way controller. The browser navigates to the website.

*Figure 4: Browser Menu*

# 3. Bookmarking a Web Page

You may add a website to your list of bookmarks to find it faster at a later date. To add a web page to your bookmarks:

1. Go to the web page you wish to bookmark. Refer to the previous section, "Navigating to a Website" on page 98, to learn how to navigate to a web page.
2. Press the **Menu** button. The Browser menu appears.
3. Select **Bookmark This Page** using the five-way controller. Push down the five-way controller. The web page is added to your bookmarks.

*Note: To learn how to view your bookmarks, refer to the next section, "Viewing Your Bookmarks".*

# 4. Viewing Your Bookmarks

Bookmarks can be stored for faster access to previously visited web pages. To view your list of bookmarks:

1. Press the **Menu** button. The Browser menu appears.
2. Select **Bookmarks** using the five-way controller. Push down the five-way controller. The list of bookmarks appears, as shown in **Figure 5**.
3. Select the web page from the list of bookmarks using the five-way controller. Push down the five-way controller. The web page opens.

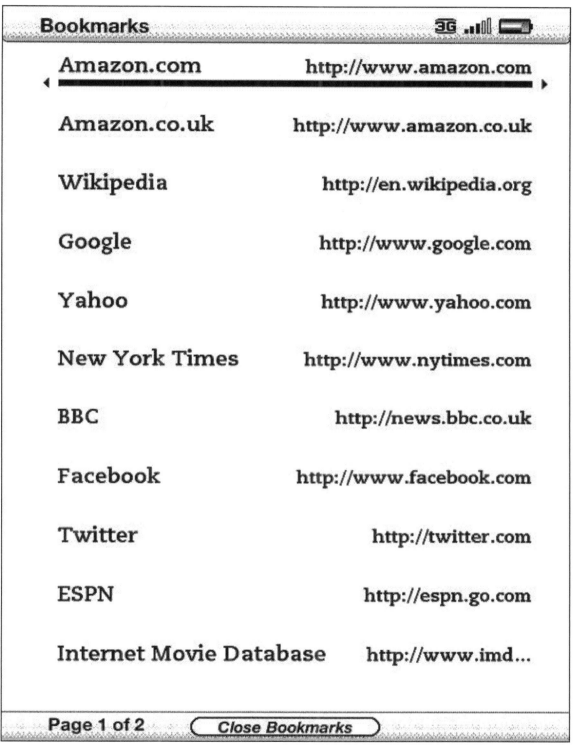

*Figure 5: List of Bookmarks*

## 5. Viewing a Recently Visited Website

The Kindle stores recently visited websites in its browsing history. To view the history:

1. Press the **Menu** button. The Browser menu appears.
2. Select **History** using the five-way controller and push down. A list of all recently visited websites appears.
3. Select a website using the five-way controller and push down. The website opens.

## 6. Clearing the Browsing History

You may clear the list of recently visited websites. To clear the browsing history:

1. Press the **Menu** button. The Browser menu appears.
2. Select **Browser Settings** using the five-way controller and push down. The Browser Settings screen appears, as shown in **Figure 6**.
3. Select **Clear History** using the five-way controller and push down. The browsing history is cleared.

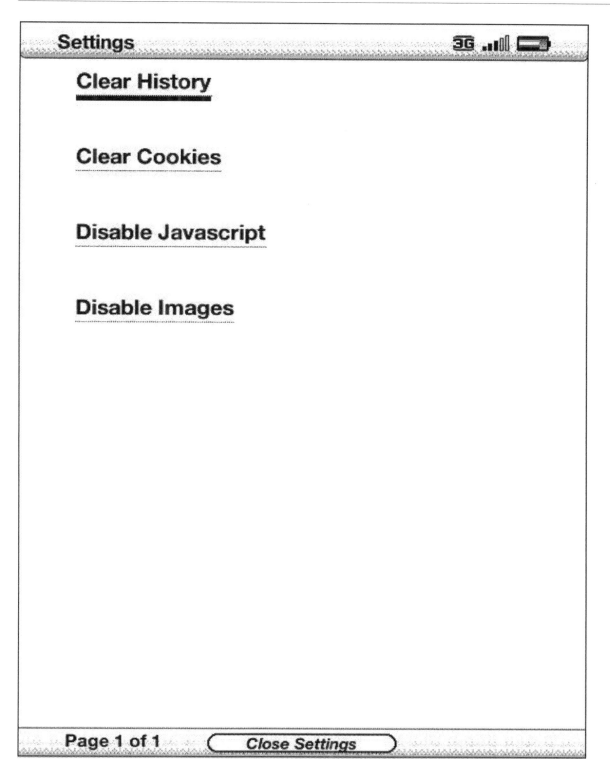

*Figure 6: Browser Settings*

# 7. Clearing Cookies

The Kindle also stores other data, such as saved passwords, called cookies, which can be cleared to free up memory. To clear the cookies:

1. Press the **Menu** button. The Browser menu appears.
2. Select **Browser Settings** using the five-way controller and push down. The Browser Settings screen appears.
3. Select **Clear Cookies** using the five-way controller. Push down the five-way controller. The cookies are cleared.

# 8. Turning on Wireless

To use the web browser, you must turn on Wireless on your Kindle. To turn on Wireless from the Home screen, press the **Menu** button. The Main menu appears. If the first option is 'Turn Wireless Off', wireless is already turned on. Otherwise, select **Turn Wireless On** using the five-way controller and push down. Wireless is turned on as long as it is available in your area.

*Note: You may choose to use Wi-Fi if your model supports it. To learn how to set up Wi-Fi, refer to "Setting Up Wi-Fi" on page 17.*

# 9. Disabling Javascript and Images

You may disable Javascript, which is used to load certain forms and other content. You may also disable images, which will prevent all images from showing while browsing. If either one of these is disabled, pages will load faster, but you will not see some of the content. Use these settings while viewing text-only web pages. To disable Javascript or images:

1. Press the **Menu** button. The Browser menu appears.
2. Select **Browser Settings** using the five-way controller. Push down the five-way controller. The Browser Settings screen appears.
3. Select **Disable Javascript** or **Disable Images** using the five-way controller. Push down the five-way controller. Javascript or images are disabled.

# Music, Games, and More

## Table of Contents

## 1. Loading Music onto the Kindle

MP3 files can be loaded onto your Kindle. To load music onto your Kindle, connect the Kindle to your computer using the provided USB cable. Open **My Computer** and open the Kindle folder on

a PC or double click the ▒▒▒▒ icon on the desktop of a Mac. The Kindle folders appear. Open the music folder. Drag and drop music into the music folder.

*Note: Refer to "Connecting the Kindle to a PC" on page 10 or "Connecting the Kindle to a Mac" on page 11 to learn more.*

## 2. Listening to Music

To listen to music on your Kindle at any time, press **Alt** and **Space** (**Alt+Space**) simultaneously. One of the songs on your Kindle begins to play.

Press **Alt** and **F** (**Alt+F**) simultaneously to go to the next track. Press **Alt+Space** again to pause the music.

Use the volume controls on the bottom of the Kindle to adjust the music volume.

# 3. Playing Minesweeper and GoMoku

To play Minesweeper on your Kindle, press **Alt, Shift**, and **M** (**Alt+Shift+M**) simultaneously. The minesweeper application opens. Use the five-way controller to navigate the squares and push down the controller to reveal a square. The goal is to mark all of the mines without stumbling upon one. The number in a square shows the number of mines surrounding it (including diagonals).

Press **M** to mark a mine. Press **R** to restart the game. Press **G** to play GoMoku. The GoMoku application opens. GoMoku is a version of the popular Connect Five game.

# 4. Using the Kindle as a Calculator

To use the Kindle as a calculator, enter any mathematical expression in the search field at the Home screen. In addition to arithmetic, you may use the following expressions:

- **sqrt** - Typing sqrt(9) would yield 3.
- **power(^)**- Typing 3^3 would yield 27.
- **Trigonometry, including: sin, cos, tan, atan** - Typing sin(90) would yield roughly 0.89, the sine of 90 radians. The number you type in parentheses is not in degrees.

# 5. Buying Applications for the Kindle

The Kindle can run applications, such as productivity programs and games. To buy an application for the Kindle:

1. Press the **Menu** button. The Kindle Storefront opens.
2. Start typing to search for an application by name. Push the five-way controller down. The Kindle searches for the application.
3. Select **Popular Games & Active Content** at the Kindle Storefront to browse applications. A list of the most popular applications appears.

*Note: Applications and eBooks are both purchased the same way. Refer to "Buying an eBook on the Kindle" on page 22 to learn more.*

# Tips and Tricks

## Table of Contents

## 1. Capturing a Screenshot

To capture a screenshot at any time, simultaneously press **Shift**, **Alt**, and **G** (**Shift+Alt+G**). The screen is stored on the Kindle as an image. You may access the image by connecting your Kindle to a computer. Screenshots are stored in the 'documents' folder. Please note that the Kindle sometimes fails to take the screenshot if you let go of any of these three buttons at any time or if you do not press Shift first. If the screenshot does not show up in your 'documents' folder after connecting the Kindle to your computer, disconnect the Kindle and retake the screenshots.

## 2. Refreshing the Display

If the Kindle freezes or is having trouble displaying the current screen, refresh the display by simultaneously pressing **ALT** and **G (Alt+G)**.

## 3. Displaying the Time and Date

To display only the time, press the **Menu** button. To display both the time and the date, press **Del** to make the search field appear. Type **@date** and push down the five-way controller. The time and date appear. Press **SYM** to type an '@'.

## 4. Displaying Available Memory

To display the amount of memory remaining on your Kindle, press the **Menu** button. The available memory is displayed at the top left of the screen.

## 5. Accessing the Amazon Kindle Store Quickly

To open the Amazon Kindle Store without going through the Kindle menu, simultaneously press **Alt** and **Home (Alt+Home)**.

## 6. Showing Available Shortcuts

You may view a list of shortcuts from the Home screen. These shortcuts are usable in any search field. Press the **Del** key at the Home screen to make the search field appear. Type **@help** and push down on the five-way controller. A list of shortcuts appears. Press **SYM** to type an '@'.

## 7. Navigating to a Web Page via URL from the Home Screen

You may quickly navigate to a URL from the Home screen. Press the **Del** key to make the search field appear. Type **@url**, press the spacebar once, and then type the URL. Push down the five-way controller to navigate to the URL. The web page opens in the web browser.

# 8. Conserving Battery Life

The following tips will help you to maximize your Kindle's battery life:

- Turn off wireless when you are not using it. To turn off wireless, press the **Menu** button at any time, select **Turn Wireless Off**, and push down the five-way controller.
- Recharge the battery when it is more than 20% charged. In other words, try not to let it drain completely before recharging it.
- Do not charge the battery to full every day. Anywhere between a 20% and 80% charge is best for this type of battery.
- Avoid exposing the Kindle to extreme hot and cold, as this will decrease the battery life.
- Put the Kindle to sleep when not using it for a short period of time. Otherwise, turn it off. Slide the power switch to the right and release immediately to put the Kindle to sleep. Slide the power switch to the right and hold it until the screen is blank to turn it off.
- Use your computer to purchase eBooks. Using wireless to purchase content directly from the Kindle uses up battery life more quickly.

# 9. Viewing an Online Article as an eBook

While reading a news article on a website, such as CNN, you may view the text in Article Mode, which allows you to use the Previous Page and Next page buttons for navigation. Press the **Menu** button while reading an article. Select **Article Mode** using the five-way controller. Push down on the five-way controller. The article is displayed in Article Mode.

# 10. Viewing an Image in Full-Screen

While viewing an eBook or other media, zoom in on an image to make it display in full-screen mode. To view a full-screen image:

1. Select the image using the five-way controller. A magnifying glass appears in the middle of the image.
2. Push down the five-way controller. The image is displayed in full-screen mode.
3. Push down the five-way controller again. The Kindle displays the full page.

## 11. Adding a Quick Bookmark

A bookmark can be added without going through the Book menu. To quickly add a bookmark, simultaneously press **Alt** and **B** (**Alt+B**). The bookmark is added and the top right corner of the page is folded over.

## 12. Starting and Stopping Text-to-Speech Quickly

Text-to-Speech can be started and stopped without going through the Book menu. The book must be compatible with Text-to-Speech. To start Text-to-Speech, simultaneously press **Shift** and **Sym** (**Shift+Sym**). The Shift button is at the bottom left corner of the keyboard. To pause Text-to-Speech, press the spacebar. Press **Shift+Sym** again to turn off Text-to-Speech. Text-to-Speech finishes the current sentence and stops.

## 13. Navigating a Periodical Quickly

Quickly navigate through a periodical by moving the five-way controller left to go to the previous article or right to go to the next article.

## 14. Clearing the Search Field

You may delete all the characters you have typed in a search field at one time. To clear the search field, simultaneously press **Alt** and **Del** (**Alt+Del**).

## 15. Entering Search Terms

While searching, do not type in a piece of a word. Always type the whole word or phrase you wish to find. Doing this will allow for much more accurate searching.

# 17. Searching the Dictionary from the Home Screen

You may look up a word in the dictionary from the Home screen. Press the **Del** key to make the search field appear. Type **@dict**, press the spacebar once, and then type the word you wish to look up. Push down the five-way controller to look up the word.

# 18. Searching the Web from the Home Screen

You may look up a word or phrase on the internet from the Home screen. Press the **Del** key to make the search field appear. Type **@web**, press the spacebar once, and then type the word or phrase you wish to look up. Push down the five-way controller to look up the word or phrase.

# 19. Searching the Store from the Home Screen

You may look up a word or phrase in the Amazon Store from the Home screen. Press the **Del** key to make the search field appear. Type **@store**, press the spacebar once, and then type the word or phrase you wish to look up. Push down the five-way controller to look up the word or phrase.

# 20. Searching Wikipedia from the Home Screen

You may look up a word or phrase in Wikipedia from the Home screen. Press the **Del** key to make the search field appear. Type **@wiki**, press the spacebar once, and then type the word or phrase you wish to look up. Push down the five-way controller to look up the word or phrase.

# 21. Using the Hidden Image Viewer

There is a basic picture viewer on the Kindle. To use the Kindle's built-in image viewer:

1. Connect the Kindle to your computer using the provided USB cable. Refer to "Connecting the Kindle to a PC" on page 10 or "Connecting the Kindle to a Mac" on page 11 to learn more. Open **My Computer** and open the Kindle.
2. Right-click anywhere on white-space in the folder. Select **New>Folder**. Name the folder **pictures** and press enter.
3. Open the pictures folder. Right-click anywhere on white-space in the folder. Select **New>Folder**. Give the folder a name and press **Enter**. The name you gave the folder will be used as the eBook name.
4. Copy pictures into the sub folder (the folder you created within the 'pictures' folder). Supported formats are JPG, PNG, and GIF.
5. Make sure the pictures have finished transferring. Disconnect the Kindle from the computer.
6. Press **Alt+Z** at the Home Screen. A new eBook appears in your Kindle library with the same title as your sub-folder.
7. Open the eBook to see your pictures. If you do not see the eBook, it may be on a different page. The images may take a while to open, depending on the size of each image.
8. Use the **Previous Page** and **Next Page** buttons to navigate the pictures. Additional pictures appear.

*Note: If you do not follow steps 1-4, you will not be able to use the image viewer and pressing Alt+Z will have no effect.*

The following is a list of image viewer shortcuts:

F: - Toggle full-screen mode

C: - Toggle actual size

Q: - Zoom in

W: - Zoom out

R: - Rotate

E: - Reset zoom level

*Note: Some of these shortcuts will not work with certain images, especially if they are of a high resolution.*

# Converting Documents to Kindle Format

The Kindle supports unprotected Mobipocket books (PRC or MOBI), plain text files (TXT), and Amazon's proprietary, DRM-restricted format (AZW). The Kindle can play the following audio files: MP3 and Audible (AA, AAX). Kindle DX also supports PDF files. Text-to-Speech, however, does not work with PDF files. To view your PDF documents and use the Text-to-Speech feature on the Kindle 3, convert them to the PRC format. There are several ways to convert your documents to the Kindle's native format.

## Table of Contents

1. Converting Files through Amazon for a Fee - easiest, the converted documents are sent directly to your Kindle.
2. Converting files through Amazon for free - easy, the converted documents are sent to your email.
3. Converting files using Mobipocket eBook Reader on your Windows PC (free) - easy, but requires downloading and installation of software on your PC.
4. Converting files using Mobipocket eBook Creator on your Windows PC (free) - requires more time investment in the beginning but provides you with most options.

# 1. Converting Files through Amazon for a Fee

Amazon provides a service to easily convert documents to Kindle's native .AZW format through email. The service is free if the converted file is sent to your established Kindle email address. The service costs 15 cents per MB if the document is sent to your Kindle wirelessly via Whispernet. Amazon can convert the following formats:

- Microsoft Word (DOC, DOCX)
- HTML (HTML, HTM)
- Text (TXT)
- PDF
- JPEG (JPEG, JPG)
- GIF
- PNG
- BMP

You can convert multiple documents at once if sent in a .ZIP file (no more than 100 documents at a time). Amazon will unzip the files and send the converted files back.

This service is fast and reliable. The converted documents are returned within 10 to 20 minutes. The title of the converted documents is constructed from the filename of the original file. Your email address is used as the author's name (for example, "john@gmail.com"). For some complex PDF and DOCX files, Kindle formatting can differ from the original.

To use this service, you need to set up your Kindle's email address at www.amazon.com/myk. In the Your Kindle section, click **Edit Info**. In the Kindle Email Address text field, change the first part of the email address to what you would like it to be. The @kindle.com will automatically be appended. Click **Update information** to save your changes and close the text entry box. Your Kindle email is now set.

You also need to set up approved "From" email addresses at www.amazon.com/myk In the 'Your Kindle approved email list' section, enter the email address and click **Add Address**. Your Kindle will only receive converted files from email addresses you have approved to prevent spam. Attach your document to a new email or forward an existing email that has a document attached to your kindle email (John@kindle.com). A subject is not necessary.

## 2. Converting Files through Amazon for Free

Amazon provides a service to easily convert documents to Kindle's native .AZW format through email. Amazon can convert the following formats:

- Microsoft Word (DOC, DOCX)
- HTML (HTML, HTM)
- Text (TXT)
- PDF
- JPEG (JPEG, JPG)
- GIF
- PNG
- BMP

You can convert multiple documents at once if sent in a .ZIP file (no more than 100 documents at a time). Amazon will unzip the files and send back the converted files. The service is fast and reliable. The converted documents are returned within 10 to 20 minutes. The title of the converted documents is constructed from the filename of the original file. Your email address is used as the author's name (for example, "john@gmail.com"). Some complex PDF and DOCX files Kindle formatting can differ from the original.

To use this service, you need to set up your Kindle's email address at www.amazon.com/myk. In the 'Your Kindle' section, click **Edit Info**. In the 'Kindle Email Address' text field, change the first part of the email address to what you would like it to be. The @kindle.com will automatically be appended. Click **Update information** to save your changes and close the text entry box. Your Kindle email is now set. You also need to setup approved "From" email addresses at www.amazon.com/myk. In the 'Your Kindle approved email list' section, enter the email address and click **Add Address**. Your Kindle will only receive converted files from email addresses you have approved to prevent spam.

Attach your document to a new email or forward an existing email that has a document attached to this email: YourName@free.kindle.com. For example, if your kindle email is John@kindle.com, then to convert files through Amazon for free send your documents to John@free.kindle.com. A subject is not necessary. The documents will be converted and emailed to your computer at the email address associated with your Amazon.com account log-in. You can then transfer documents to your Kindle's documents folder. Refer to "Connecting the Kindle to a PC" on page 10 or "Connecting the Kindle to a Mac" on page 11 to learn more.

# 3. Converting Files Using Mobipocket eBook Reader on Your Windows PC (free)

Mobipocket Reader is primarily used to read and organize Mobipocket format eBooks on a Windows PC and smartphones. It looks and works similar to iTunes. The Mobipocket Reader can also easily convert your documents to PRC files. Download the free Mobipocket Reader to your Windows PC from http://www.mobipocket.com/en/DownloadSoft/ProductDetailsReader.asp (there is no Mac version).

After you install the Mobipocket Reader, you can simply drag-and-drop files into the Mobipocket Reader window (You can also click the Import icon on the Navigation bar). The formats that can be converted are:

- Microsoft Word (DOC, RTF)
- Microsoft Excel (XLS)
- Microsoft Power Point (PPT)
- Microsoft Visio (VS)
- Microsoft Compiled HTML Help (CHM)
- ePUB
- HTML (HTML, HTM)
- Text (TXT)
- PDF

The converted eBooks are saved to your Mobipocket Reader library folder, located in "..\Documents\My eBooks\". The results of the conversion are similar to the Amazon server conversion.

# 4. Converting Files Using Mobipocket eBook Creator on Your Windows PC (free)

You can use the free Mobipocket eBook Creator to convert the following files to PRC format on any Windows PC:

- Microsoft Word (DOC)
- HTML (HTML, HTM)
- Text (TXT)
- PDF

The MobiPocket eBook Creator software is easy to use, the conversion is fast, and this method provides you with the most options. To transfer the PRC files to your Kindle, connect the Kindle to a USB port and copy the PRC files into documents folder on the Kindle. Any other files created during the conversion (.XML.OPF) are unnecessary and can be deleted. Note that Amazon owns the Mobipocket company, so in effect you are using Amazon's own software to generate PRC files. For best results, use well-structured HTML as a starting point. Note, that to view HTML files on the Kindle, you do not need to convert them to PRC format. Simply rename the file extension to TXT. The HTML file will appear on the Kindle Home screen.

# Working with Dictionaries

## Table of Contents

## 1. What is a dictionary?

One of the greatest features of the Kindle is its native support for dictionaries. The New Oxford American Dictionary is pre-installed on the Kindle. Open the New Oxford American Dictionary and type in any word. The alphabetical list of available articles is updated as you type a word. Select any article using the five-way controller and read the full entry. The format of the New Oxford American Dictionary is called 'dictionary format'.

The pre-installed New Oxford American Dictionary is an excellent English dictionary, but what do you do if you are reading a Spanish text? This is where Kindle shines. You can purchase a Spanish dictionary and have that Spanish dictionary work exactly like the New Oxford American Dictionary. Refer to the next section on page 119 to learn how to choose the default dictionary.

Translation dictionaries and some encyclopedias are also available in dictionary format. Unfortunately, it is often unclear whether an eBook is in dictionary format. The fact that the eBook has "Dictionary" or "Encyclopedia" in its title does not guarantee that this book is published in dictionary format. We suggest that you always download a sample eBook before buying a full version.

## 2. Choosing the default dictionary

You can choose the dictionary you want to use when looking up words in an eBook. The default is the New Oxford American Dictionary. To select a different dictionary:

1. Download a new dictionary. This can be a translation dictionary or an encyclopedia published in dictionary format, such as The Big English Encyclopedia from MobileReference. It can be in English, Spanish (such as The Big Spanish Encyclopedia from MobileReference), or in any other Latin language.
2. Press the **Menu** button at the Home screen. The Main menu appears.
3. Select **Settings** using the five-way controller and push down. The Settings screen appears.
4. Press the **Menu** button. The Settings menu appears.
5. Select **Change Primary Dictionary** using the five-way controller and push down. A list of dictionaries appears.
6. Select the dictionary you want to use. The new dictionary is selected and will be used to define words while reading.

# Troubleshooting

## Table of Contents

## 1. Kindle won't turn on or is frozen

If the Kindle freezes up or does not turn on, try one of the following tips:

- Recharge the Kindle using the power adapter (not through your computer). Make sure the orange light on the Kindle is on. Charge the Kindle for at least 30 minutes before attempting to turn it on.

- Turn the Kindle on using the power switch. If the Kindle still does not turn on, reset the device. Disconnect the Kindle from any power source and slide and hold the power switch for 15 seconds. Release the power switch. The screen is blank for 30 seconds while the Kindle resets and restarts.

- If none of these tips work and the orange light is on while charging, you may need a new Kindle battery. Contact Kindle support at **1-866-321-8851** or **kindle-cs-support@amazon.com** to resolve this issue.

## 2. Wireless isn't working or the Kindle is unable to download an eBook despite strong signal strength

Restart the Kindle by doing the following:

1. Press the **Home** button. The Home screen appears.
2. Press the **Menu** button. The Main menu appears.
3. Select **Settings** using the five-way controller and push down. The Settings screen appears.
4. Press the **Menu** button. The Settings menu appears.
5. Select **Restart** using the five-way controller and push down. The Kindle restarts.

If this doesn't work, try turning off wireless and turning it back on. Press the **Menu** button at the Home screen, select **Turn Wireless Off**, and then **Turn Wireless On**.

Also, try moving to a different area, as the signal strength may not have been updated since your last location.

## 3. Received only partial download or content is corrupt

Delete the content and download it again from Archived Items. To remove and re-download content:

1. Select the content you wish to delete using the five-way controller. Move the five-way controller to the left. 'Remove from Device' appears.
2. Push down on the five-way controller. The content is archived.
3. Select **Archived Items** at the Home screen using the five-way controller. Push down on the five-way controller to confirm. The archived items appear.
4. Select the content you wish to re-download using the five-way controller and push down. The content is re-downloaded.

# 4. Trouble transferring content from a computer to the Kindle

If you are having trouble transferring content to your Kindle, try one of the following tips:

- Connect your Kindle directly to your computer's USB port instead of a USB hub.
- If the Kindle is connected to a USB port, try a different one.
- Turn off any anti-virus software that is running on your computer.
- Turn off any active firewalls.
- Restart your computer while the Kindle is still connected and try to transfer the content again.

# 5. Text-to-speech sound is distorted

- If the sound on the Kindle is distorted, try switching between the male voice, female voice, and back.
- You may also try restarting the Kindle by doing the following:

1. Press the **Home** button. The Home screen appears.
2. Press the **Menu** button. The Main menu appears.
3. Select **Settings** using the five-way controller and push down. The Settings screen appears.
4. Press the **Menu** Button. The Settings menu appears.
5. Select **Restart** using the five-way controller and push down. The Kindle restarts.

- Play an MP3 and, if the sound is still distorted, contact Customer Support at **1-866-321-8851** or **kindle-cs-support@amazon.com** to resolve the problem.

# 6. Kindle doesn't charge using the power adapter

Make sure the orange light on the Kindle is on. If the light is not on, try another outlet. If the light is on, restart the Kindle by doing the following:

1. Press the **Home** button. The Home screen appears.
2. Press the **Menu** Button. The Main menu appears.
3. Select **Settings** using the five-way controller and push down to confirm. The Settings screen appears.
4. Press the **Menu** button. The Settings menu appears.
5. Select **Restart** using the five-way controller and push down to confirm. The Kindle restarts.

# 7. Cannot open any eBooks and an error message appears

Restart the Kindle by doing the following:

1. Press the **Home** button. The Home screen appears.
2. Press the **Menu** button. The Main menu appears.
3. Select **Settings** using the five-way controller and push down to confirm. The Settings screen appears.
4. Press the **Menu** button. The Settings menu appears.
5. Select **Restart** using the five-way controller and push down to confirm. The Kindle restarts.

If restarting does not help, perform a factory reset. To perform a factory reset:

***Warning: All files except for eBooks are permanently deleted during a factory reset. Back up any documents, periodicals, and MP3's before resetting.***

1. Press the **Home** button. The Home screen appears.
2. Press the **Menu** button. The Main menu appears.
3. Select **Settings** using the five-way controller and push down. The Settings screen appears.
4. Press the **Menu** button. The Settings menu appears.
5. Select **Reset to Factory Defaults** using the five-way controller and push down. The Kindle resets to factory defaults.
6. After the reset is complete, you may re-download your content from the Archived Items. After downloading, the content is restored.

# 8. No sound can be heard

If there is no sound coming from the Kindle's speakers, try turning up the volume using the volume control on the bottom of the Kindle. Also, make sure nothing is plugged in to the headphone jack.

If using headphones, plug the headphones all the way in. The speakers are disabled when the headphones are plugged in.

## 9. Cannot connect to Whispernet

To connect to Whispernet, wireless must be turned on and you must have a signal of at least one bar. To turn on wireless, press the **Menu** button at the Home screen, select **Turn Wireless On**, and push down the five-way controller. Wireless is turned on.

## 10. Kindle is broken and a replacement is needed

If your Kindle is completely broken (i.e. if too much pressure is placed on it, the screen may break), call **1-866-321-8851** and choose **option 3**. Have your Amazon account information ready. After answering a few questions, the customer support representative may offer to replace the Kindle at no extra charge to you, apart from the shipping charge to send the old Kindle back to Amazon. A shipping slip will be sent via email. Take this slip and your Kindle to a local UPS store to ship it. The shipping cost will vary, but will not be more than several dollars.

## 11. What to do if your problem is not listed here

If you could not resolve your issue, contact customer service using one of the following methods:

If you are in the U.S., call **1-866-321-8851**.
If you are outside the U.S., call **1-206-266-0927**.
Email Kindle at **kindle-cs-support@amazon.com**
Visit **http://www.amazon.com/kindlesupport**.

# Kindle Survival Guide from MobileReference

## Author: Toly K
## Editor: Julia Rouhart

**This book is also available in electronic format from the following vendors:**

- **Amazon.com**
- **Barnesandnoble.com**
- **iBooks for iPhone and iPad**

MobileReference is a brand of SoundTells, LLC.
Please email questions and comments to support@soundtells.com. Normally we are able to respond to your email on the same business day.

MobileReference®. Intelligence in Your Pocket™.

## *Praise for the* Kindle Survival Guide

"Like many new Kindle users, I bought this 'survival guide' when I first logged into my Kindle account. The very first tip that I used was a tip on downloading free eBooks. That repaid the cost of the 'survival guide' right away. Was this information available elsewhere? Definitely, and those with plenty of time will find it. But if you want to save time, then this guide is for you.

My next task was to familiarize myself with the Kindle interface. Again, the 'Survival Guide' served its purpose. It directed me through the multiple capabilities of the Kindle step-by-step. Who knew that the Kindle had games, that it can be used as an image viewer, and as a calculator? I did not see the instructions for any of these capabilities in the official Kindle Manual. Now I am able to read free news from the Kindle web browser and use Kindle to send an occasional email."

*S. Goldberg*

"After trying to read the eBook manual that came with the Kindle, I realized it was written like a novel rather than a how-to user guide. This is probably why people don't read manuals. The Kindle Survival Guide was simple, to the point, and broken up into chapters to make information very easy to access. There is no technical jargon and the required actions to complete each task are clearly outlined. What a great reference tool."

*J. Hessman*

"I have always loved to read and have owned the Kindle for quite some time. However, I have only used the reading function. After the new Kindle came out, I gave my old one away and bought the new one. To get the most out of the third generation Kindle, I bought this book, since it was the most popular guide for the Kindle 3.

In addition to new features, I discovered that what I thought I already knew about the Kindle can be done with greater efficiency. I found out about many new shortcuts after reading this guide. For example, I learned how to start and stop text-to-speech with a two-key combination, allowing me to turn my eBooks into audiobooks and read on the go with no hassle. This guide was written for book lovers."

*C. Mackenzie*

## *Other Books from the author of the Survival Guide Series, Toly K*

*iPad*

*HTC Incredible*

*Samsung Droid Fascinate*

*iPad 2*

*Nook Color*

*Sony Reader*

*iPhone 4*

*How to Find & Download Free eBooks*

*iPad Apps for Scientists*

*Galaxy Tab*

*Droid X*

*Kobo*

HTC Droid 4G

iPad Games for Kids

iPhone

Nook

Xoom

# Notes

Made in the USA
Charleston, SC
04 November 2011